CW01573074

2007

A POETRY ODYSSEY

After a voyage of 2,500 years, poetry has finally reached the stars ...

Verses From Cheshire
Edited by Claire Tupholme

 Young**Writers**

First published in Great Britain in 2007 by:
Young Writers
Remus House
Coltsfoot Drive
Peterborough
PE2 9JX
Telephone: 01733 890066
Website: www.youngwriters.co.uk

SB ISBN 978-1 84602 820 5

Foreword

This year, the Young Writers' *2007: A Poetry Odyssey* competition proudly presents a showcase of the best poetic talent selected from thousands of up-and-coming writers nationwide.

Young Writers was established in 1991 to promote the reading and writing of poetry within schools and to the young of today. Our books nurture and inspire confidence in the ability of young writers and provide a snapshot of poems written in schools and at home by budding poets of the future.

The thought, effort, imagination and hard work put into each poem impressed us all and the task of selecting poems was a difficult but nevertheless enjoyable experience.

We hope you are as pleased as we are with the final selection and that you and your family continue to be entertained with *2007: A Poetry Odyssey Verses From Cheshire* for many years to come.

Contents

SS Peter & Paul Catholic College, Cheshire

Callum Whatley (14) 1
David Simpson (13) 1
Sean Myler (13) 2
Jenny Colquitt (13) 2
Sarah Bedwell (13) 3
Hannah Conway (13) 3
Jessica Grainger (14) 4
Laura Hessey (13) 4
Daniel Cleary (14) 5
Liam Donnelly (13) 5
Joe Burke (14) 6
Alex Paton (13) 6
Michelle Murphy (13) 6
Olivia Langton (13) 7
Chloe Campbell (13) 7

St Chad's Catholic High School, Runcorn

Lois Mercer (13) 8
Sarah Hancox (13) 8
Becky Cornes (13) 9
Amy Moore (13) 9
Jordan Holmes (13) 10
Charlie Forshaw (13) 10
Laura Murphy (13) 11
Kieran Shepherd (13) 11
Jodie Burns (13) 12
Sarah Steele (13) 13

Sale High School

Thomas Fletcher (11) 13
Joseph Clover (12) 14
Amy Riding (11) 14
Jack Bingham (11) 15
Greg Nicholson (11) 15
Jordan Badger (11) 16
Katie Dixon (11) 16
Chelsey Phelan (11) 16

Alex Williams (11)	17
Jamie Worsley (11)	17
Bethany Murphy (11)	17
Jade Hand (12)	18
James O'Brien (11)	18
Louise Guerrieria (11)	18
Josh King (11)	18
Bobbie Wilde (11)	19
Adam Smith (12)	19
Tom Hendley (11)	19

Tarporley Community High School

Oliver Baker (11)	20
Matthew Magee (11)	20
Ben Tyler (12)	21
Thomas Sarstedt (11)	21
Lauren Heath (11)	22
Charlotte Slattery (11)	22
Murray Russell (11)	23
William Lewis (11)	23
Florrie Kirby (11)	24
Lucy Rogers (13)	24
Catherine Bull (11)	25
George Kirby (13)	25
Ashleigh Dean (11)	26
Liam Crabtree (11)	26
Harriet Redman (11)	27
Dan Thomas (13)	27
Emily Harris (14)	28
Charlotte Malyon (11)	29
Natalie Sefton-Fiddian (13)	29
Sophie Jones (12)	30
Alex Andrew (14)	30
Harry Heath (13)	31
Alexandre Gilchrist-Jones (13)	31
Amy Jones (13)	32
Sophie Spencer (11)	32
Megan Jones (13)	33
Alice Grindley (13)	33
Katrina Whitehead (13)	34
Callum Lowe (14)	35

Natasha Drinkald (13)	35
Natalie Wilson (13)	36
Molly Horsman (13)	37
Charlotte Nichols (14)	38
Cam Watson (13)	38
Emily Hill (13)	39
Megan Wood (13)	40
Isabel West (12)	40
Sally Rowley (14)	41
Alison Tough (13)	41

The Bankfield School

Kelly-Anne Mitchell (12)	42
Aaron McGarvey (13)	43
Toni Jackson (13)	44
Jessica Faulkner (12)	44
Georgia Durr (13)	45
Christopher Power (12)	45
Adam Baldwin (16)	46
Jonathan Radley (13)	47
Sam Burton (13)	47
Gemma Egan (14)	48
David Sweeting (12)	48
Samantha Mercer (12)	49
Stacey Clark (15)	49
Danny Barrow (13)	50

The Kingsway School

Bethany Hudson (12)	50
Roselyn Chigerwe (13)	51
Lewis Behan (12)	51
Josh Seddon (12)	52
Lewis Johnson (12)	53
Ben Cuthbertson (13)	54
Matt Boyd (13)	54
Sahar Fallaha (13)	55
Arakit Puri (13)	55
Abigail Beckett (13)	56
Barney Miles (13)	57
Oliver Parr (13)	57
Rebecca White (14)	58

Katie Rebecchi (14)   59
Daanyal Naveed (13)   59
Charlotte Peers (13)   60
Michelle Hill (12)   61
Katie Strong (12)   62
Jenny Parkin (13)   62
Abbie Gibson (11)   63
Benjamin Henderson (11)   63
Nazanen Sadati (12)   64
Katie Collins (11)   64
Baber Uppal (11)   65

The Queen's School
Charlotte Newton-Hale (11)   66
Georgina Bolwell (11)   67
Jill Evans-Higson (13)   68
Elisabeth Welburn (11)   69
Katherine Lewis (11)   70

Tytherington High School
Helen Simmons (12)   71

Upton High School
Joseph Craig (12)   72
Charlotte Parry (12)   73
Vanessa Ellis (12)   73
Lucinda Dodd (12)   74
Katherine Burt (12)   74
Chloe Seville (13)   75
Gareth Lilley (13)   75
Alex Perratt (13)   76
Oliver Barnett (13)   77
Leah Lipscombe (12)   78
Hasna Ali (12)   79
Rachael Brierley (13)   80
Natasha Hickson (12)   81
Byron Forster (14)   82
Mia Gatward (13)   83
Ian Wilson (13)   84
James White (12)   85
Lauren Riley (12)   86

Alexandra Terry (17)	87
Lewis Whitehouse (12)	88
George Welsh (12)	89
Daniel Preston (12)	90
Imogen Rhodes (12)	91
Francesca Walton (12)	92
Ellie Liddell-Crewe (12)	93

Verdin High School

Martin Clarke (11)	93
Emily Pointon (12)	94
Mark Robson (11)	94
Adam Smith (12)	95
Yasmin Woodward (11)	95
Danielle Harris (11)	96
Ben Littlemore (11)	97
Samantha Lyon (11)	98
Molly Grogan (11)	99
Kayleigh Daniels (12)	99
Jade Vernon & Warrick George (11)	100
Emily Baddeley (11)	100
Jacques Vincent (11)	101
Kavan Farrell (11)	101
Kelly Davenport (13)	101
Chloe Sharrock (11)	102
Molly Carroll (11)	102
Elliot Orme (11)	103
Chloe Bell (11)	103
Daniel Munro (11)	104
Jessica Hughes (12)	104
Charlotte Ellis (11)	105
Jack Oakes (11)	105
Emily Williams (11)	105
Leann Brown (12)	106

Weaverham High School

Jarrod Pickering (11)	106
Chris Dilnot (11)	107
Will & Sam Monson (12)	107
Luke Basnett (11)	108
Gemma Craven (11)	108

Carys Tavener (11)	109
Olivia Done (12)	109
Melissa Brown (11)	110
Liam Hampson (11)	111
Laura Foy (11)	111
Mark Marafko (11)	112
Rachel Trafford (12)	112
Sarah Gerrard (11)	113
Joe Dalton (12)	113
Jessica Dean (11)	114
Natasha Jackson (12) & Amanda Harris	114
Oliver Timmins (11)	115
Lucy Moulton (11)	115
Sarah Koch (11)	116
Farrah Hallworth (12)	116
Will Jordan (11)	117
Toni Woodward (11)	117
William Corradine (11)	118

Werneth School

Shaun Scott (13)	118
Jessica Porter (12)	119
Alex Moore (12)	119
Lauren Baguley (12)	120
Rio Trowsdale (12)	120
Thomas Welton (13)	121
Alexandra Wilson (12)	121
Bradley Walker (12)	122
Sean Bowen (12)	122
Megan Burns (12)	123
Toni Crosby (12)	123
Jake White (12)	124
Bradley Fuller (12)	124
Katie Spencer (12)	125
Coral Heavyside (13)	125
Amber Marsland (12)	126
Jake Francis (12)	127

The Poems

A Secret

I told my mate a secret,
Unfortunately he didn't keep it,
He betrayed me in every way,
I got harassed the next day.

They skittled me and joked around,
Last week I thought they were sound,
I want to forgive him now,
But I just don't know how.

I'm gonna forgive him today,
But I still don't know what to say,
So I went up to him and said, 'It doesn't matter mate
Everybody makes mistakes!'

Callum Whatley (14)
SS Peter & Paul Catholic College, Cheshire

Betrayal

The story of the Tempest,
Is an interesting tale,
It includes romance,
And a lot of betrayal.

Once the king was shipwrecked,
He dealt with betrayal,
Because instead of rescue,
His fleet continued to sail.

Caliban served Prospero,
But secretly planned betrayal,
It would have worked if he was sober,
But he got drunk and so did fail.

David Simpson (13)
SS Peter & Paul Catholic College, Cheshire

Magic

Magic is fun, magic is harsh,
From witchcraft to wizardary,
From evil to good,
Magic could,
Make you rich,
Make you poor,
Give you power,
Give you more,
Make you suffer,
Make you tougher,
And give you luck.
But before you read the magic book,
Be careful or you will be shook,
By the harsh world of magic!

Sean Myler (13)
SS Peter & Paul Catholic College, Cheshire

Fear, Fate

Your heart is pumping faster and faster,
You are scared this will be a disaster,
As your fate draws closer to you,
Your conscience tells you things to make you renew,
The things you told yourself before you did it,
To make you think, why did I do it?
But that doesn't help you know the end is near,
Here it is . . .
You are filled with fear.

Jenny Colquitt (13)
SS Peter & Paul Catholic College, Cheshire

What Is A Friend?

A friend is someone who gives you a smile,
A friend is someone who sticks around for a while
A friend is someone that tells you no lies,
A friend is someone who always tries.

A friend is someone who will give you a moment,
A minute, an hour.
In times of need they are your tower.
A friend is a shoulder, a hand, a rock,
Whatever you need isn't a shock.

So if you're a friend remember
What I say,
Because one day soon you
Will need a friend this way.

Sarah Bedwell (13)
SS Peter & Paul Catholic College, Cheshire

Friend

My friend makes me smile,
When I am feeling down,
Never laugh at but with,
Never judge but encourage.
They understand when you think they shouldn't,
Birthdays, Christmas, pass,
But they're always there for you.

Hannah Conway (13)
SS Peter & Paul Catholic College, Cheshire

Mysteries Of The Past

The red glove hangs on the schoolyard fence,
The owner's hand, long a thing of the past,
Once a warm, comforting shelter,
From the chilled wickedness of winter,
Now home to its children,
Snow, hail and a splintered glass frost.

I see this scene every day,
A piece of our community; an accepted sight of our town.
Yet our blissful ignorance prevents us,
From asking questions whose answers don't need to be found.

Will the other still be found?
Reunited after pasts apart.
To whom did it once belong?
The importance of those five fingers,
Were they powerful, were they strong?

What did life hold for them?
Were they dealt a good hand?
Did they have a head start
Or struggle with misery and sin?

I ask these questions
Yet I regret that it has been too long,
Loud silence,
The past has been and gone.

Jessica Grainger (14)
SS Peter & Paul Catholic College, Cheshire

Magic

Mythological magic and wizardry spells
Made up stories and fairy tales.
Tempests, storms and violent gales.

Laura Hessey (13)
SS Peter & Paul Catholic College, Cheshire

No More Slaves

A flash of light
From Prospero's staff
So bright it lit up the whole night
Suddenly after you heard a laugh.

A crash of thunder
From the sky
I saw a boat go right down under
On the seabed where it lies
No one appeared to have died.

A massive snap, a plunging sound
Prospero's staff hit the ground
His book all wet
He shan't forget
How much he loved that sound
When the broken staff hit the ground.

No more slaves
A stoppage of waves.

Daniel Cleary (14)
SS Peter & Paul Catholic College, Cheshire

Magic

Pick up the magic wand
Get your wizards and form a band.

All together we can make a spell
So that others will be so jealous, they yell.

Go and get a duck from the lake
Stir it round and add some cake
Put in a frog with only one eye
Stir it round and put in an owl with red dye!
Spit in a big huge spit
And then throw in a footie hit
Stir it round, click, shout, pop, crackly, clang,
Bang!

Liam Donnelly (13)
SS Peter & Paul Catholic College, Cheshire

Farewell

My life is ruled by torture and pain,
Nothing has fought me and not been slain.

Yet, although nothing seems to faze me,
All this fighting has driven me crazy.

I destroy my foes with animosity,
They look on at me like I'm a monstrosity.

All my years enslaved as a captive,
My life wasn't exactly interactive.

My blood, sweat and tears created this cataclysm,
Where will I find the strength to make this final incision?

Into the body of someone I know all too well,
Now is the time to say farewell . . .

Joe Burke (14)
SS Peter & Paul Catholic College, Cheshire

Mystical Magic - Haiku

Alakazam, poof!

Wizards, witches, waving wands.

Mystical magic!

Alex Paton (13)
SS Peter & Paul Catholic College, Cheshire

Lies - Haiku

Lies and deceiving
Anything but the trust, just
Lies and deceiving.

Michelle Murphy (13)
SS Peter & Paul Catholic College, Cheshire

Magic

A wave of a wand
A flash of a stick
A few books and potions
A magic trick.

A rabbit, a toad
Or a little black cat
Simply pulled
Out of a magical hat.

A disappearing act
Rings of fire
Levitating tricks
Lifting you higher.

Abracadabra
Alacazzoo
Magical words
Make dreams come true!

Olivia Langton (13)
SS Peter & Paul Catholic College, Cheshire

What Magic Can Do!

A crash of thunder,
A spark of light,
A terrible storm all through the night!
Pick up your staff,
You begin to laugh,
Look what you've done!
You've finally won!
You've cast your spell,
Then people fell,
You love your magic,
No matter how tragic,
It can be,
To you or to me!

Chloe Campbell (13)
SS Peter & Paul Catholic College, Cheshire

Missing You Badly, Missing You Sadly

This poem is for my mum,
Whose happy face reminded me of the sun.
Her features were perfect,
They made people swoon with the effect.
The way she flicked her golden hair,
To see it untidy was very rare.
Innocent, blue, gleaming eyes,
You could tell she told no lies.
The lips that were so gentle to touch,
Oh! I miss her so so much!

Her make-up was always just right,
Never too dark, yet never too light.
Taking care with the perfume she chose,
Smelling delicately with her sweet little nose.
Ears that could hear a pin drop,
And even the smallest slightest pop.
Getting her nails done every Tuesday,
Until of course that day in May.
It was a cold day,
In the car was me, Mum and our Faye.
The car slid on the ice,
What happened next was not very nice.
I miss you Mum, I miss you badly,
I miss you dearly, I miss you sadly.

Lois Mercer (13)
St Chad's Catholic High School, Runcorn

My Love Poem

When I am with you I feel so right
When I am without you my love for you is tight.
When I feel alone, until I come home, you are there at the door,
But I love you no matter what.
I'll love you forever.

Sarah Hancox (13)
St Chad's Catholic High School, Runcorn

Untitled

I awoke to the sweet sound of birds singing,
The gentle scent of flowers wafting through my window.
I lay there for a while,
Not stirring and not sleeping,
But drinking in the beauty by which I was surrounded.

I slipped out of bed and opened my door,
I headed down the long flight of stairs,
And found myself emerged in a riot.
The singing of birds was engulfed by raucous voices,
And I felt myself going dizzy at the sight.

Like a gunshot's effect, the room went silent in her presence,
The toys stopped playing, the children stopped running.
Her footsteps were akin to an elephant
And her voice boomed around the room.

Every morning I would wake up in peace,
Surrounded by beauty, the shimmering sea not far.
No sooner would I have woken, but to realise the
Reality of it all, the riot downstairs was a regular occurrence
In this place.
This place where I am held.

Becky Cornes (13)
St Chad's Catholic High School, Runcorn

Poem

Bonfire Night is a time
When rockets set off into the sky
The pop and bang
Crowds of people look up to see the flash
The colours are refreshing and very pretty too
They bounce out of the sky and fade away through the night.

Amy Moore (13)
St Chad's Catholic High School, Runcorn

The Pathway

I am the pathway
I don't like it when people walk on me
And I hate it when people throw sticky stuff all over me
It just looks a mess.

The other day some little boy
Was riding his bike on me,
He kept doing skids on me
And leaving thick black marks on me.
Unfortunately he fell off.
His mum came over and started smacking me
Saying, 'Naughty path!'
Hitting me as if to say it was my fault.

He shouldn't have been going so fast!
Served him right.

Jordan Holmes (13)
St Chad's Catholic High School, Runcorn

My Love Poem

When I'm with you
You make my heart swell up
Like an air balloon
But when I'm not
No matter what you do
I will always love you.

We might have a fight tonight
But no matter what
You will always be

My loving light.

Charlie Forshaw (13)
St Chad's Catholic High School, Runcorn

The Popular Girl

She came into school with not one hair out of place,
And make-up slapped on that delicate face.
One click of a finger and the world was hers,
There she is, right in the centre of all the chairs.

Blonde hair, blue eyes,
Oh I could go on forever.
Perfect boyfriend, perfect smile,
The list never ends.

I loathe her and her pretty head,
'Look at the stage of her,' I said.
'Why is she always so perfect?' I sighed,
It doesn't even look like she tried.

Why oh why can't they see,
That she is just the same as you and me.
She eats not a thing,
I mean look at her bling!

Life is all diamonds and things,
Just look at them platinum rings,
But I bet you there is a story behind that smile,
After all, the mirror doesn't lie.

Laura Murphy (13)
St Chad's Catholic High School, Runcorn

Big Bully

I am rolling down town
I give someone a frown
People think I am hard
But really I play them like a pack of cards.

Kieran Shepherd (13)
St Chad's Catholic High School, Runcorn

The Street With No People

No shadow to follow
No traffic to whir,
This street has no people,
No people to stir.

The houses all crooked
The dark things at bay,
This street has no people
No people who stay.

The empty street's calling
But nobody's there
This street has no people
No people who care.

The trees loom over
And whisper into the night
This street has no people
No people in sight.

The stars ahead whisper
At these great goings on,
This street has no people
The people have gone.

The sun comes up
And I slink away,
In this street with no people
Is where I shall stay.

Jodie Burns (13)
St Chad's Catholic High School, Runcorn

Musings

Who am I but a
Dreamer
Residing in a land of dreams.

Who am I but a
Thinker
Of a million mystifying thoughts.

Who am I but a
Wisher
Of so many hopeless desires.

Who am I but a
Drifter
On wings of imagination.

Who am I but a
Daydreamer
Living in my own world.

Sarah Steele (13)
St Chad's Catholic High School, Runcorn

Lemmings - Haiku

Lemmings oh lemmings
They are suicidal ha
They live in my game.

Thomas Fletcher (11)
Sale High School

My Favourite Show

Wrestling is my favourite show,
My favourite is Mysterio.
Batista is my second best
Better than all of the rest.

Undertaker I just hate!
He probably rarely gets a date.
Kennedy isn't far behind,
'Cause he's just got a messed up mind.

In November is the best
Survivor Series beats the rest.
Cena, Batista I don't know
But Mysterio will win the show.

Joseph Clover (12)
Sale High School

Spring

It is the first day of spring,
Hear the birds sing,
All of a sudden the snow has gone,
And as for the stars, there are none.

Now the snow is gone, the plants can grow,
Farmers in the fields, seeds to sow,
The sun is out, the sky is blue,
There is not a cloud to spoil my view.

See the joys that spring brings,
Lots of new and wonderful things.
The animals love it when it is so hot,
We have enjoyed the spring such a lot.

Amy Riding (11)
Sale High School

Spring

New bulbs begin to flower,
As down comes the April shower
Blossom fills the trees
As new life begins to breed
Baby birds hatch
And frogspawn we try and catch
Little lambs skip and jump
Across the fields farmers clump
And as the birds twitter and sing,
You see it's here . . . spring.

Jack Bingham (11)
Sale High School

My Pet

I once had a hamster called Freddy
He reminded me of a teddy
He lived in a cage
And he was brown and beige
He had fluffy bedding,
And had an imaginary wedding.
When I cleaned his cage out,
He used to mess about.
I put him back in his bed to be fed
And then it was time for bed.

Greg Nicholson (11)
Sale High School

Hallowe'en

H appy people all around
A ll people having fun
L ots of people are scared
L aughing children are so loud
O wls hooting is a scary sound
W hining babies all around
E veryone can hear no sound
E vil spirits flying around
N ow Hallowe'en is over.

Jordan Badger (11)
Sale High School

My Family

My family are so annoying,
Yes, that's right, my brother and sister.

Forgiving, funny, forgetful and frightening,
Active, wild, crazy and bonkers,
Mentally mad, but kind and caring,
Ignorant sister, only sometimes,
Loving and laughable,
Yep, that's mine.

Katie Dixon (11)
Sale High School

My Girls!

I look at my friends then I look at me
Without my hunnys where would I be?
My friends, my sisters, my shadows, my world,
Where would I be without my girls?
Tears, giggles, smiles and laughs,
Late night calls and cute photographs.
I'll be there for you until the day of my death,
Best girlies forever till my very last breath.

Chelsey Phelan (11)
Sale High School

War Poem

As the rifles fire,
Many troops tire,
Many foes, muscles
Are flopping and
They are dropping
As we come out of
The door,
We notice we've
Won the war!

Alex Williams (11)
Sale High School

Money, Money

Money in my hand
To buy all the things I want,
One million pounds.

Green, green money
The smell makes me funny,
I don't know why
It's just my tummy!

Jamie Worsley (11)
Sale High School

Chocolate - Haiku

Choc, choc, chocolate
White, dark, milk, what do you like?
They all melt so nice.

Bethany Murphy (11)
Sale High School

Popcorn - Haiku

Popcorn sizz-er-ling
On this wonderful hot day
So come and join me.

Jade Hand (12)
Sale High School

Ice Cream

Ice cream cold and white
It looks nice and bright
Eat on a dark night.

James O'Brien (11)
Sale High School

Toenails - Haiku

Horrible toenails
On the end of my big toes
Are yellow and long.

Louise Guerrieria (11)
Sale High School

Italy - Haiku

Italy is big,
Italy shaped like a boot
Alps are there for you.

Josh King (11)
Sale High School

Shopping - Haiku

Shopping is so great
I buy all the things I want
Getting things in town.

Bobbie Wilde (11)
Sale High School

Fire - Haiku

Spreading in the air
Bigger it grows run get out!
I can't escape now!

Adam Smith (12)
Sale High School

Bogeys - Haiku

Big, nasty bogeys
Up both of your big nostrils
Pick them out today!

Tom Hendley (11)
Sale High School

My Teacher Thinks . . .

My teacher thinks I am learning my flags
But, really I am having 4 o'clock tea with the Queen,
I am swimming with dolphins in America,
I am protecting England with the Royal Navy.

My teacher thinks I am checking my homework
However, in real life I am diving into a chocolate sundae
I am flying on a broom with Harry Potter,
I am on a mission and working for MI6.

My teacher thinks I am a writing a story
But, really I am standing on a giant gingerbread man,
I am camping with the England football team under the Eiffel Tower,
I am flying over the moon on a flying pig.

My teacher thinks I am reading a book
However, in real life I have gone back in time and I am
Helping build the Great Wall of China,
I am in Ireland learning how to Riverdance,
I have won the final of Big Brother and Davina McCall is
Interviewing me.

My teacher thinks I am getting ready to go home
But really my mind is in another world altogether.

Oliver Baker (11)
Tarporley Community High School

War In The Skies

Through the skies they soar,
Like an eagle or a hawk,
Flying for their lives, determined,
To do their duty.
Twisting and turning trying to get the enemy in their sights.
One plane is going down, on fire and burning.
Planes circling round and round,
Only half a squadron coming back
The next day facing death again.

Matthew Magee (11)
Tarporley Community High School

Medieval Massacre

Dedicated warriors march to their graves,
Sweaty hands, clutching metal blades.

Blood rushing to their fingers,
While their hair pricks on the back of their necks.

Metal meets metal, in a deathly slice,
Blood and guts gushing from bodies,
Smell the rotting insides.

The cavalry enter, with a thunder of hooves,
Archers let fly their arrows, piercing beating hearts,
Massive boulders drop from the sky.

The river dyed with dark red blood,
Horses sink to the depths.

Finally the battle ends
No one wins, everyone's dead.

Ben Tyler (12)
Tarporley Community High School

The Roman Killers

Fearless warriors marching out to no-man's-land,
The cavalry clutching the reigns on their steeds,
Archers grasping the wooden bows with sweaty hands,
Soldiers charge in a full force stampede,
Axes, clubs, swords and spears all ready to kill,
Some soldiers have already been squashed dead,
Suddenly screams everywhere,
Guilty soldiers make their first kill,
Hopeless warriors give up and die,
Arrows rain down on people,
Three days later nothing of value is left,
You can smell and see the rotting blood and guts,
Discarded weapons left on the floor,
The grass is red with blood,
No point in this war just to gain power.

Thomas Sarstedt (11)
Tarporley Community High School

Friends

Friends forever
Friends you can't forget.

Everybody needs a friend now and again.

There are best friends, special friends, but
Most of all there are friends.

We have old friends and new.

Friends will be there on your wedding day,
Your birthday and when you need them most.

Friends are people you would never change.

Friends are people you will always have memory of.

Friends are happy and sad.

Remember friends are there for life.
Remember.

Lauren Heath (11)
Tarporley Community High School

Dancing!

I love to dance,
The moves I do are fast,
I dance to all kinds of music,
Mostly dance music,
I practise in my room,
And sometimes teach my friends the dances I've made up,
Dancing is fun,
I wear comfortable clothes to dance in,
Everyone should try dancing,
Because dancing is fun!

Charlotte Slattery (11)
Tarporley Community High School

The Stories Of The World

If you look at the river,
You'll see a dark shape in the water,
And you'll hear a slither,
If you look in the sky,
And you really try and look very high,
You'll see a bird fly into a tree and die.

There's a dragon in the mountain caves,
Who enjoys a cauldron of mushroom soup,
Whenever the shiny blue moon happens to wave,
There's a tribe in Nambia deserts,
Greeting one of their own kin,
When dark brown arrows rain like water on them.

Deep under the deep dark sea,
There's a loud fun party on the ocean floor,
For a monkfish that just turned 104,
There's a lot of stories all round the world,
And you can tell them even if you're young or old.

Murray Russell (11)
Tarporley Community High School

Space

I sat on a seat in the rocket,
The ground shook uncontrollably,
My head stuck to the back of the seat as I went up,
After a while I took my seat belt off and I floated around
                                    the grey spaceship,
When we landed I floated out of the ship,
I was stood on the moon,
I was cold but there was no wind,
I saw pitch-black for miles,
Every now and then I saw a star twinkle,
The floor was cold and hard,
But suddenly my rope snapped
I slowly floated away,
I called for help until my radio signal went . . .

William Lewis (11)
Tarporley Community High School

Moggy

My cat Moggy,
Is a cheeky cat.
Once she even caught a bat,
And left it on the kitchen floor,
Till my mum kicked it out the door.

My cat Moggy,
Is a sneaky puss.
She often sneaks under a bus,
But always comes out the other side,
Even though they are very wide.

My cat Moggy,
Is a lovely pet.
She fell in the pond and got all wet,
Though she drives me round the bend,
I love her till the very end!

Florrie Kirby (11)
Tarporley Community High School

My Hero

My goodness you're fast
All you see is a red and black blur go past,
Loud noises, screams, engines roaring,
Vibrations run through my body,
You're 5th coming up,
Now you're 3rd, you've done a big jump,
Crowds screaming,
Come on, you can do it,
Your car's fast enough!
Your foot's to the floor,
You're in the slipstream,
Now go!
You're brave and courageous,
You are my hero, a winner,
You rock
        Tom Chilton!

Lucy Rogers (13)
Tarporley Community High School

The Race

Standing on the block,
Nervous to the bone,
Here goes the whistle,
Its terrifying moan.

Throwing myself off,
Into the deep blue,
Soaring through the water,
I'll catch you!

I'm halfway there,
Swimming front crawl,
Splish, splash, splosh,
I'll beat you all!

End of the race,
Hooray I won!
Celebrate together,
Have lots of fun.

Catherine Bull (11)
Tarporley Community High School

School

Hey diddle duddle
My mind's in a muddle
I cannot think what to do,
The teachers all laughed
And said I was dumb,
Not my fault I haven't a clue!

Hey tiggle toggle
My mind's in a boggle
My writing is going askew
I'm looking so daft
And feeling so glum
I think I'll be copying you!

George Kirby (13)
Tarporley Community High School

Netball

Jump for the ball,
High as the sky,
Into the net,
The ball does fly.

Yes, we are winning,
One nil up,
Now I am thirsty,
Reach for the cup.

Now we are playing again,
Pass me the ball,
Careful Charlotte,
Please don't fall!

The ball comes to me,
I need to shoot,
Please go in,
Or I'll get the boot!

Now it's the end
Hooray we won,
I have to go,
Here comes my mum!

Ashleigh Dean (11)
Tarporley Community High School

South America

Condors lurch on the treacherous rock
In South America it's 5 o'clock.

Lizards scramble on the desert floor
People in Peru extremely poor.

The Amazon river shining bright
The rainy season out of sight.

Liam Crabtree (11)
Tarporley Community High School

Lulu

Lulu my pony,
So loving and cute,
Riding her is fun,
Then I feel we've won.

Going to school
Without saying bye,
Thinking of her,
As she gallops by.

I see her in pink,
And then I think,
A coloured pony
Is Lulu.

On a winter's day
I have to say
When I give her a feed
She hates the weed.

Harriet Redman (11)
Tarporley Community High School

The Long Road

The long, cold, steamy road,
The trees shiver,
As they moan,
The hustling of bushes,
The scream of haunted animals,
They moan and tremble at night.
The stream still trickles,
The moon shines bright.
The stars still sleep,
The darkness of the sky!
Scuttling noises of animals
The long road.

Dan Thomas (13)
Tarporley Community High School

Things Change

When I was young
My father took me on holiday
To see the Disney Parade.

I said, 'When I grow up, could I be
Minnie Mouse
In the Disney Parade?'

He said, 'You can do anything
If you believe in yourself.'

The whole of my childhood
I dreamed about becoming
Minnie Mouse
In the Disney Parade.

When it came to the time
When I had to choose a career track
To follow
I forgot all about my childhood dream.

I chose to become a teacher
So I could work with children.

On a school trip we went to Disneyland
To see the Disney Parade.
I then remembered my childhood dream
I remembered how much I wanted to be
Minnie Mouse.

Isn't it strange how your dreams change!

Emily Harris (14)
Tarporley Community High School

The Fair!

Ferris wheel big and high
Ferris wheel touch the sky

Horses bright, merry-go-round
Circus music, loud sound.

Candyfloss light and fluffy
Furning air hot and stuffy.

Litter fills the ground
Rides are turning all around.

Crowded fun house, magic spark
Lights go off now in the dark.

Laughing clowns, hamster wheel
Hook a duck, get a deal.

Bumper cars ready to mash,
Bumper cars raring to crash.

Hot dogs fill the air
Massive ride, waiting stair.

Fair so fun, beer bottles lie
But now it's time to say goodbye.

Charlotte Malyon (11)
Tarporley Community High School

Hit And Run

Pedestrians cross the road,
Cars speed through the country lanes,
Night soon falls
Only one pedestrian crossing, the death trap,
Only one car skimming the highway,
Only one death
One close escape
And another hit and run.
No one can help when the dark is about.

Natalie Sefton-Fiddian (13)
Tarporley Community High School

My Family Thinks

My teacher thinks I'm doing my maths,
But actually I'm swimming with dolphins,
My friend thinks I'm at my house,
But really I'm locked in a store cupboard in Japan,
My mum thinks I'm tidying my room,
But I'm sipping tea with the Queen,
My dad is sure that I'm watching TV,
But I'm actually feeding penguins in the Atlantic.

My brother thinks I'm at school,
But I'm writing down the new law for Tony Blair,
While my dog eats its lunch,
I'm at the Bafta Awards sitting next to Girls Aloud,
My grandma believes I'm painting in the living room,
But I'm actually walking the Great Wall of China,
My teacher thinks I'm cooking but really
I'm in another world altogether.

Sophie Jones (12)
Tarporley Community High School

My Poem

Manchester United are the best,
They are better than all the rest,
They will beat rubbish Liverpool,
That is because Man U rule.

Rooney and Ronaldo make a great team,
But Peter Crouch, that height I've never seen,
We have a good keeper to stop the shots,
That's because he practices lots.

But overall it's just a lot of fun,
I'll play every day till the setting sun.

Alex Andrew (14)
Tarporley Community High School

The Baby

It was a mistake
Your father, he is a fake
He said was nice
But he had headlice
We had both planned a party
But your daddy did a farty
So everyone got up to leave
Your father and me conceived
Nine months later I was in labour
But I suppose your dad did me a favour
He helped me make you
Even if you always poo
And now it's your birthday
Look at the present from your aunt May
You were my special present from your dad
But he was a very naughty lad
He used to hit me black and blue
I was scared he might just turn on you
But now you're safe, you won't get the shove
I will always show you, eternal love.

Harry Heath (13)
Tarporley Community High School

Skateboarding

I am interested in skateboarding,
It is as fun as wakeboarding,
A make is called Blind,
I think you will find
When you hit the floor you'll whine.

My favourite shoes are Vans,
I walk around the street kickin' cans,
I look for a place to grind,
I think you will find,
It's harder than it looks!

Alexandre Gilchrist-Jones (13)
Tarporley Community High School

The Crime Scene

The trigger has been pulled,
The bullet is on its way
Someone is going to have
A guilty conscience on this day.

Everyone is shouting,
Hell is in the room
People started screaming
Because they heard the boom.

People lying on the floor,
Trying to hide their heads
Everybody's very scared
Lots of blood has been shed.

The criminal starts running off,
From this crime scene
Sirens call and police rush in
To see who has been

Handcuffs are upon him,
The man that committed this crime
Everybody is thinking the same
Lock him away and make him do his time.

Amy Jones (13)
Tarporley Community High School

Animals

A nimals are very loving things
N o one ever hates them
I n the holidays you can go to see them in zoos and lots
more places
M ammals are a type of animal, the ones who are most like humans
A nimals most of the time eat each other for their prey
L ots of animals like to have their own space to live in
S o that's my poem on animals!

Sophie Spencer (11)
Tarporley Community High School

Remember This . . .

Take care in life
Enjoy it while you are young
Look after yourself.

Remember . . .
Today is the first day of the rest of your life,
So do something or make something happen
That is different to yesterday.
Live everyday to the full.
We are not here as long as we
Would like to be.

Tell someone they look nice today
And make them feel good
It will make you feel good too.

If you love someone, tell them
Hearts may be broken by words
Left unspoken.

Remember this . . .

Megan Jones (13)
Tarporley Community High School

True Love

You fell from the sky just like a star
That's what I wished and here you are.
You make me laugh, you make me smile,
The wish I made was worthwhile.
True love is hard to find.
Special 1-1 of a kind.
But the love inside of me is true,
And it appeared today when I met you.
I feel that you are the key to my heart.
I don't think I could stand it if we were apart.
But if we are I will write your name in the sky,
So the whole world can see that you are mine.

Alice Grindley (13)
Tarporley Community High School

It's Christmas Time

It's almost Christmas, the trees are up
Everyone's full of joy,
Laughing and smiling all day long,
Thinking of the newborn boy.

It's Christmas Eve, it's all tradition,
Roast chestnuts with mulled wine,
Singing carols round the fire,
The children's eyes did shine.

Children not wanting to go to sleep,
Too excited for Christmas Day,
Waiting for Santa to come with their presents,
They know he's on his way.

The children are drooping almost asleep,
Too tired to stay up and wait,
A kiss goodnight, tucked up tight,
They know it's really late.

Almost Christmas morning, nearly time to celebrate,
The 25th of December
A happy joyful day.

Finally the day has arrived
Oh yes it's finally here,
The day of celebrating, giving and receiving,
Without an inch of fear.

But don't forget the lonely or old,
Who could be on their own,
Sitting at home looking at memories,
Thinking of people they've lost and now been left alone.

The day has gone, until next year,
We will celebrate the newborn birth.
With happiness and laughter,
Because of what it is worth.

Katrina Whitehead (13)
Tarporley Community High School

Crewe Alexandra FC

The Premier league is here
The Crewe fans sing and cheer
The mighty Reds win every game
All the Crewe fans are badly insane
Crewe Alexandra are in town
They make the opposition look like clowns
Dano Gradi is our king
Also David Vaughn on the left wing
Nicky Maynard is our man
Scoring goals, that's his plan
Every game home and away
The Crewe fans sing their hearts away
The whistle starts the game
With the Crewe team full of fame.

Callum Lowe (14)
Tarporley Community High School

You!

Every night I dream of you,
All sweet, never cruel,
But that's not true,
You beat me until I'm black
And blue.

But I still love you,
As I will always do,
I remember you all sweet and
Gentle
But now you're harsh and
Mental.

There is no chance
That we will be,
Is there?

Natasha Drinkald (13)
Tarporley Community High School

Hunter Of The Shadows

As silent as a shadow
No sound does she make
Surveying her land
Far above.
Her eyes burn with fire
With the thrill of the hunt,
As her prey comes closer,
Tonight it will end.
Her face is pale,
Her lips cherry-red.
Above her shoulder,
An eye watches
Fierce and proud.
Her guardian, her soul.
The eagle swoops and dives
Razor-like talons glint
A shriek of pain,
Then silence.
The woman smiles
Cold, cruel
An evil smile.
The bird returns
The woman and the eagle,
United as one,
The hunter of the shadows.

Natalie Wilson (13)
Tarporley Community High School

Colours

The colours of the day
And night,
The colours of the dark
And light,
Red,
Yellow,
Green
And
White,
Brown,
Blue,
And
Grey.
Colours of the moods, we're in
A boring graph,
A photograph,
It's what makes
The world so great
Colours are what make
The world.

Molly Horsman (13)
Tarporley Community High School

Christmas

Everyone is full of Christmas cheer,
I'm sure it's everyone's favourite time of year.
I like the crisp, white snow,
I love the Christmas flow.
Christmas shopping is really fun,
All my bags weigh a ton.
Candy sticks, chocolate too,
Some for me and some for you
Christmas Eve at the Swan
All our worries will have gone
Walking back in the pitch-black
Some Christmas decorations look quite tack.
Christmas Day is the best
I get just as much as the rest
When Christmas Day is over
I hate it!

Charlotte Nichols (14)
Tarporley Community High School

Liverpool FC

L iverpool Football Club
I n the Premiership, that's where we are, topping the league
that's our aim
V ictory is our game
E verton, our arch enemies
R iise our left wing man
P roud of our club, that's what we are
O ver and over again we win
O ver and over, we perform over everyone
L yrics fill Anfield with atmosphere all ninety minutes

F ollowing them all the way to glory
C rouch, our attacking man, heading the ball home, all the time.

Cam Watson (13)
Tarporley Community High School

When My Brother Was Born

I was with my nan outside the room.
Nan said there will be a little boy soon.
I heard my mother scream.
I thought it was a nasty dream
I cried for my mummy.
But Nan gave me my dummy.
I heard a baby cry
Then my nan sang me a lullaby.
The nurse came in full of joy.
She said you have a little boy.
Dad came out and held me tight.
And said your baby brother will be home tonight.
Me and my dad went inside,
The room was full of joy and pride.
Mum told me his name was Matt
It doesn't get better than that.
Mum put Matt into my lap
And there he lay and had a nap.
We just stared at each other,
Just me and my little brother.
My brother was born that day,
I love him more than words can say.

Emily Hill (13)
Tarporley Community High School

Hope

He left the house without a sound,
On his selfish journey into town.
In his head this was all OK,
But to us it wasn't, he'd lost his way.
-      The pills had taken over.

She stood all alone in the corner of school,
Children jeered and yelled they can be so cruel.
'No one can help me' she thought to herself,
How long would she sit all alone on this shelf.
-      Could she just jump off?

They stared and stared into each other's eyes,
Her soulmate was not like all the other guys,
No words were spoken but still he knew,
The tragic end this could come to.
-      Army life will sacrifice love.

Hope, through adversity shines ever strong,
The journey is brutal and painfully long.
But faith in our heart will guide us through all,
Belief in a bright future has a very clear call.
-      What doesn't kill you makes you stronger.

Megan Wood (13)
Tarporley Community High School

Wintertime

Winter draws in,
Leaves curl up,
Soft velvet carpet layered on the ground,
Snowflakes falling from the still night sky,
Frozen water glimmers in the moonlight,
Watch the children having fun,
Snowmen stand,
Proud and still.

Isabel West (12)
Tarporley Community High School

I Love You

Those are the words of a million feelings,
I whisper them to your heart.
Those simple words you know so well
I've loved you from the start.

No one else in the world can compare,
You're perfect and so is the love we share.
In your eyes I see our future, in your eyes I see our past,
By the way you look at me I know our love will last.

The first time we met, I could see,
That you and I were meant to be.
Your eyes so gentle, your smile so true,
When you first held my hand, I just knew.

A bond so strong, a hold so tight,
To know you're the one, my Mr Right.
A blessing sent from up above
In you I've found my one true love.

Sally Rowley (14)
Tarporley Community High School

Autumn

The fading lush green of summer long gone, new colours emerge
Yellows, reds, oranges, make up the colours of trees
Animals go into hibernation, even the busy bees.

A new wilderness is coming to life
With badgers, birds, foxes and deer
It's getting colder now with winter near.

Leaves swirling in the strong wind
Rain starts to pour
I put on my wellies and raincoat and open up the door

I splash around in the puddles
I'm having so much fun
But I must go now, my clothes are wet, it's not much fun for
Mum.

Alison Tough (13)
Tarporley Community High School

Donny Scanlon

I am now in jail
And now I can't get bail
So please help me escape.

I was driving at night
There was an awful fright
I swerved across the road.

I hit a car
I swerved very far
And then I ran away.

I killed two men
A boy was ten
I put him in a wheelchair.

He thought it was me
When he glanced at me
So he stalked me.

And then he found out the truth
I thought my plan was foolproof
So I bribed him not to tell.

And here I am
Sitting on a bed
Feeling sad
Not at all glad
Feeling sorrow
Feeling bored
Here I am ten years more.

Kelly-Anne Mitchell (12)
The Bankfield School

Liverpool FC

Come around to the
Magnificent ground
And watch the best football
Around.
Watch the ball get passed all
Round the ground.
Hear the sound of the ground
When the ball hits the back of the goal,
They won the Champions League
Five times in the ground of
Istanbul,
And eighteen titles of the greatest
League around.
If you want to join the mighty
Reds come on down the Anfield
Ground,
And help the Kop sing around
The ground.
So come on down to the
Magnificent ground
And watch them pass the ball
Around,
That's what you call the
Greatest team around.

Aaron McGarvey (13)
The Bankfield School

Love Is A Mystery

Love is a mystery that can't be solved,
Cupid fires an arrow and arguments are resolved.

There is only one key that can open the heart,
It belongs to the angels and it's drawn in their art.

Fairies soar and pixies run,
Matchmaking is lots of fun.

The midsummer's sun has gone away,
The mystery won't be solved for another day.

All the creatures great and small
Have worked together through it all.

The mystery has been solved today,
Cupid's children have come out to play.

Love isn't a toy, love isn't a game
When you fall in love, it will
Never be the same.

Toni Jackson (13)
The Bankfield School

Life

The world's your oyster
As you sail across the sea

The moon, the sun, anything
You want to be.

Shop till you drop with the money you earn
Or do something you wished
You had done.

All in all what I am trying to say
Is that there's always going to be
Another day.

Jessica Faulkner (12)
The Bankfield School

Teacher's Pet

Teacher's pets are squirts and a soppy bore.
If there's any homework they're always asking for more.
Teacher's pet is a sneaky git.
They always do their bit.
As the day comes to an end
I walk round the bend,
Walking home on the street,
And listening to my heart beat.
When he turned up
With Coke in his cup
By the way my name's Ken
He comes round with his beefy breath.
He left me alone for some reason . . .
Being
He was giving another boy a wedgie
Oh well
It wasn't me
Ha-ha.

Georgia Durr (13)
The Bankfield School

The Chair Of Steel

Imprisoned and stranded in the chair of steel
With rusted wheels that are cold to feel.
Who would love this monstrous beast,
Trapped inside the cold leather seat?
Running and playing had now been ceased,
The dream of winning a sprinting medal
Had now been shattered by the Devil.
Oh cruel fate why have you bestowed
Upon me this chair of steel with
Rusted wheels that are cold to feel.

Christopher Power (12)
The Bankfield School

A Social Curse

Sitting in a corner, a toy on a shelf,
I hear you laugh, I hear you live.
You try to hurt me, so I won't be myself,
Does it frustrate you, to know I won't give?

You think that it must hurt me,
Never to party in the night.
It is by choice, that I stay in after tea,
For when I'm alone, I smile and take flight.
I'm free!

You think that it's everything, just to be cool,
You bully, you skit, you dictate.
How is it that you can't see that you are a fool,
With a hunger for acceptance you'll never sate.

Alone in the night, I never cry,
Because my mind is flying free.
In a Utopia world, across an infinite sky,
Now do you see? You'll never understand me.
I'm alive.

This world is mine, so pure and so fine.
I know how to give, I've learnt how to live.
You think I should hide, yet I'm happy inside
I'm not that one who's insecure, I know this for sure;
I'm different from you, we can all see that's it's true. But . . .
I'm happy.
Are you?

Adam Baldwin (16)
The Bankfield School

Everton FC

Come on down
To the Everton ground
And watch them pass the ball
Around.
You can watch them play footy
And they might get a little
Lucky.
You can sit in all the stands but
If you are bad you will get banged.
My favourite stand is Park End Stand
No one really gets banned.
The Everton ground is called
Goodison Park and there's a lot of bark
When the ball is in the back of the net
But why do that when
You can just place a bet.
We are seventh in the League and
Having a good season
That is why you should come on down
To the Everton ground.

Jonathan Radley (13)
The Bankfield School

The Killer

I sit in a jail all on my own dreaming of my life before!
I'm in the cold and sit in dirty grime!
I think of what happened if the grizzly incident hadn't occurred!
When I stepped into court I saw them,
They're the families of my victims!
When the hammer came down he shattered my life as well!
Now I sit in a cold dark cell wishing, my life could restart!
Now the boy is paralysed!
His dad is gone and he'll never ever return!

Sam Burton (13)
The Bankfield School

Musical Instruments

Musical instruments are all in a range of sizes,
Humungous, mediocre and minuscule.
Fascinating!
You can play them cool!

You can either be a complete disaster,
Just plain average; or a master.

You don't have to use sheet music, just play it off by heart,
Don't forget, music is an art.

Play in an orchestra, ensemble or just as a solo,
So pick your instrument and make a start.

Plenty to choose from, there's quite an array,
Just start playing then you're up, up and away.

Gemma Egan (14)
The Bankfield School

The Wheelchair

W heeled about everywhere
H elped by all
E xternally injured and I want to
E scape. I
L ong to run with my best friends
C hase my friends in the park. I
H ate to sit while I watch my friends. I want to feel the
A ir in my hair as I run with my friends
I want to play well
R un and shout, but the wheelchair. I'm in a wheelchair.

David Sweeting (12)
The Bankfield School

Being Bullied

I feel terror, I feel fright
Every day I'm in a fight
They hit me, skit me all day
Help me someone, they won't go away.
No one cares for what they say.
They get me to do things which I don't know.
But if I don't do it that's when it starts, all this
Bullying has gone too far.
So I will go now and I'll be happy
Down in my grave where they can't get me.
So now you know what bullying can do to someone
If it happens let someone know 'cause
If you don't the bullying will grow.

Samantha Mercer (12)
The Bankfield School

You And I

First time I saw you, I knew something was there,
Even now when you hug me, I know you still care.

You still make me breathless, when you smile,
I feel like my heart, just ran a mile.

I love us being together, you and I
Being parted or away from you, I want to cry.

You make me feel special and a true friend,
I would never want this feeling to end.

So much time has now passed,
It's one thing I know will last.

You and I.

Stacey Clark (15)
The Bankfield School

The Angry Lion

There once was a lion that lived in Rory Lane
He had a friend called Fred that wasn't very tame
Fred teased the other lions and pushed them on the ground
He bullied people in school and robbed from the lost and found.

The lion that lived on Rory Lane was sick of Fred's behaviour
He told his mum and dad and they got even graver
His mum and dad went up to Fred and told him to be good
Fred didn't listen and pushed them in the mud.

The mum and dad were very muddy so went back to Rory Lane
To think of a cunning plan to get Fred good again
The clock struck three and they had a brilliant plan
To get Fred to say sorry if they can.

They went up to Fred and told him off
Fred said sorry and said, 'You're the boss.'

After all the hassle everything was better
Fred was kind and was as weak as a feather.

Danny Barrow (13)
The Bankfield School

Friends

A friend should always be there,
Through the good times and the bad.
To always make you happy, when you're sad
They always tell the truth, if they like what you wear.

What is a friend,
If you can't fall out.
To make you want to scream and shout,
The things that twist you round the bend.

A best friend is forever,
It means never saying bye.
Sitting down together, watching the hours fly.
A friendship forgotten never.

Bethany Hudson (12)
The Kingsway School

I Want You To Know

A little moment of darkness was that I knew before
Heaven's gate came into my view. Loved ones and
Companions I had thought of for many years
Welcomed me with open hearts and many happy tears.

All the hurt, fear and pain that I have ever known
Has gone from my life and I am finally home.
I looked upon the Lord's smiling face and for the first time in my life
I knew and felt his grace.

A cool breeze on your face, a touch of light and rain
I will send as a reminder that we will be reunited again.
Life on Earth is one brief moment in time
And I am finally home.
Eternity is mine.

Roselyn Chigerwe (13)
The Kingsway School

Game Over

Green grass
White lines
Roaring crowds
Skilled players
Flashy boots
Pristine kits
Silly haircuts
Sweaty bodies
Running legs
Flying ball
Goalie misses
Goal disallowed
Rubbish referee
Game over.

Lewis Behan (12)
The Kingsway School

The Pickled Squirrel

There were two old tramps called Rob and Jim,
Who were very fond of bottles of gin,
They spent all day drinking in the park,
They were there for hours until it was dark.
Rob was a big man with lots of hair,
Jim was a Scouser, small and fair,
Tales they would tell to one another,
Of when they were young and got into bother,
One summer's day when it was particularly hot,
Both fell asleep in a shady spot,
Whilst in a deep sleep they did not see,
A squirrel looking upon them from the tree,
Down it came with a mighty grin,
And off it went with their bottle of gin,
Into the branches with a flurry,
It drank all the gin in a hurry,
The squirrel started to stagger, its head in a spin,
It lost its balance and dropped the gin,
'Argh!' screamed Rob as he woke with a fright,
Rubbing his head with all of his might.
He looked down to see what had hit him,
And there on the floor was the bottle of gin,
He stood up and screamed, ' What have you done Jim?
I can't believe you've drunk all our gin!'
'It wasn't me, I promise, I swear!
But I bet it was you, you great ball of hair!'
They started to argue, they started to fight,
They pushed and they punched with all of their might.
Unbeknown to them above in the trees,
The squirrel swayed with wobbly knees,
Down it fell, in a drunken haze,
And there it lay in a complete daze,
The squirrel was spotted by Rob and Jim,
Who suddenly realised what had happened to their gin!

Josh Seddon (12)
The Kingsway School

London To Edinburgh

From platform number one
To leave London
To go to Edinburgh
In four hours - four hundred miles.

The guard: 'All aboard!'
A hiss, a jolt, a chug
And slowly we move
Out of platform one, London.

Shovel coal, shovel coal,
The fire burns hot yellow.
A rising tower of steam and smoke,
As the mighty, metal engine pulls.

The long, twisty rails wind
Through the countryside.
Dividing the meadows,
Sleek and streamlined, the train races north.

Nearing the end, we slow.
Steam off. Brakes on.
The couplings tighten.
The carriages jolt and groan.

Grinding to a halt,
Platform three, Edinburgh.
The guard: 'All change!'
Doors fling open, out we come.

Lewis Johnson (12)
The Kingsway School

Feel The Cold Winter Wind?

Feel the cold winter wind?
Whistling across rooftops,
Slamming against doors,
Sending a chill through the rafters.

Can you see the snowflakes?
Gently twirling down in spirals,
Slowly, but surely filling up driveways,
Clogging up alleys and roads.

See the thin crisps of ice?
Little would you know,
Strong enough to wreck mayhem,
Yet it melts between my palms.

Coating everywhere with this white coat
From the highest mountain
Down to the lowliest plains,
During the cold of winter.

Just as the snow starts to set
A stream of light shines,
Rising the temperature
And then winter ends.

Ben Cuthbertson (13)
The Kingsway School

Getting Old!

Feeling old and always tired?
Soon you will be retired!
Sitting around all day long
Then again, I may be wrong!
You might start gardening,
Or playing squash.
You may become rich 'n' posh!
I've no idea but either way,
You'll be old anyway!

Matt Boyd (13)
The Kingsway School

Autumn

Below the grey, dull sky,
The wind was whistling and whispering.
The rain was tears dripping down,
Making puddles like splotches of black paint
Poured on the ground.

The rustling leaves whirled in the wind
Like orange, red and yellow
Pieces of card being tossed everywhere.

Breaths of cold wind hit against my ears.
Leaves ran in circles around my feet.
Drops of rain rolled down my spine.

Then, the clouds walked across the grey sky,
To let the sun peek through,
And everything became brighter,
And the scene was like a painted picture.

Sahar Fallaha (13)
The Kingsway School

Outer Space

Over 10,000 million years
Up in the sky far, far away
The solar system formed.
Earth was the one with people
Revolving around the sun.

Supernovas making colossal explosions
Phases of the moon in the sky
Auroras display dazzling light.
Constellations appearing in the sky
Eclipses accrue, taking our light away.

Arakit Puri (13)
The Kingsway School

Autumn!

Warm bonfire colours blaze;
Covering the ground like a devil's red carpet.
Floating, hovering, painfully dying,
Humungous horse chestnut trees stand firm,
With their roots sucked to the floor.
Towering like a gigantic turret, protecting.
Conkers are cannonballs
Shooting from the trees in their spiky sockets,
Acorns lay half-eaten whilst mischievous squirrels
Chatter and giggle.
Children hustle and fight a war;
Until somebody has been knocked down
And has to pick up the bruised remains!
The wind blows reassuring whispers of kindness and love
Couples walk hand in hand, blinded by their hearts,
The wind rattles and shakes the trees,
Ripping them to reveal bare skin.
Raindrops patter and trickle down guarding windowpanes,
As houses pull up their coats to be warm.
The town was airbrushed in tender, cosy shades,
But now dribbles down into a pool of lava
And races down the road.
But it will return again tomorrow,
The same gust and breath of wind.
Every murmur, every rustle,
Like a never ending story . . .

Abigail Beckett (13)
The Kingsway School

Rivers

Rivers are full of beauty,
With fish and rocks and trees.
Relying on its gentleness,
From the mountains to the seas.

Rivers are full of happiness,
When you are full of joy.
An exciting place to have a swim,
A place not to destroy.

Rivers are full of sounds,
As they whisper and they whistle.
Through many woods and many towns,
Passing daffodil, rose and thistle.

Rivers are full of feelings
When you are boiling hot.
Like a glass of water in the desert,
As they cool you down a lot.

Rivers are full of structure,
They're snakes on forest floors,
Meandering around and round,
They are things you can't ignore.

Barney Miles (13)
The Kingsway School

The Slug!

As I am walking down the street,
I look down at my feet,
To find him there,
Longing, slithering, he doesn't have hair,
Green or grey I don't know,
All I know is that he moves so slow,
I'll go and get a hot water jug,
Because all I can see is this
Filthy, slimy slug!

Oliver Parr (13)
The Kingsway School

Here We Go Again

Autumn
Writhing mess of gold, red and brown
We stood on the hill
Your blue gloved hand in mine
'Beautiful,' you said
'Oh yes,' I said.
I wasn't talking about the trees.

Winter
Holly time, spiky time
Red blood, glossy green
You winked from under the mistletoe
Your present that year
A heart necklace that lies next to mine
It wasn't real gold, but it felt real to me.

Spring
New life, new chance, fresh start.
You said no and frost departs.
The shine leaves the world
Flowers push their way -
Oh so tentatively! -
Through the earth, and you stamp on them.

Summer
Grains in our beach picnic
You and me, and your more-than-friend
Sand trickled through my fingers
You slid out of reach.
So much salty water
No one noticed three drops more.

Rebecca White (14)
The Kingsway School

Autumn!

Quicker than usual,
The days turn to dark;
And Bonfire Night
Makes a spark!

The leaves fall to the ground all crunchy and crisp,
Like a white blanket covering the sky, the morning mist;
The steamed up windows, they are a kettle,
The flowers dead, every petal.

Rain beating on front doors,
Leaves brushing dirty floors;
Trees waving scratching claws,
Wind creating mighty roars.

The birds fly south to migrate,
Before snow falls and it's too late.
The green on the leaves disappear,
Once more it repeats, as it did last year.

Katie Rebecchi (14)
The Kingsway School

Get Up!

'Get up, get up!' screamed my mum
This morning.
'Get out of bed you sleepyhead'
She said as she made her bed at
7.30 this morning.

I got up to tell her that it was Saturday morning
But without a doubt she had left for work.
As she had forgotten that it
Was Saturday morning.

Daanyal Naveed (13)
The Kingsway School

Hallowe'en

Children giggle,
Pumpkins glare,
Witches cackle,
Skulls stare.
Costumes, masks,
Face paints too,
Plastics skulls chatter,
Toy ghosts whoo.
The children go to the house,
On top of the hill,
It's crumbling and empty,
It sits very still.
They go through its gates,
Up its overgrown path,
They knock on the door,
And it opens with a crash!
But there is no one there,
The children shout, 'Hello?'
But it appears that,
There is nobody home.
They turn to leave
But then someone shouts, 'Come in.
Don't worry children,
The feast is about to begin.'
So they tiptoe through the door,
But no lights are on,
And then the children disappear,
One by one.

Charlotte Peers (13)
The Kingsway School

Cold Winter's Day

Winter is here,
Christmas is coming,
Children are playing
Carol-singers humming.

Trees that are white,
Cars they glisten at night,
The cold wind blows,
As the stars twinkle like shimmering lights.

Streets are so icy, so cold
And so bright.
From the snow that sparkles,
On a Christmassy night.

People are walking
Crisp and crunch
Is the sound that it makes
As people hurry for their lunch.

Snowflakes falling
Dawn is breaking
Streets turn quiet
Now that it turns morning.

People awake
Know that it is Christmas time
Opening their presents
Adults drinking red wine.

Michelle Hill (12)
The Kingsway School

A Summer's Day

The sea swam in sunlight
As gulls flew overhead.
Beaches rocked gently,
The waves in their bed.
Roses bloomed shyly,
Kept growing in size,
As they reached with their petals,
Up to the skies.

The waves reached the shoreline,
Splashing on rocks,
Spraying the children
Who played on the docks.
And the roses sent a fragrance into the air,
So fresh and fulfilling
That none could compare.
The still and the quiet of the warm afternoon,
Belonged to contentment,
Ended too soon!

Katie Strong (12)
The Kingsway School

Snowfall

Crisp white fills the sky,
Icing the streets below.
Towering trees shiver in the wind
And the swirling drifts of snow.

Millions of flakes like confetti,
Falling for miles around.
Cocooning us in bitter cold
And lathering the ground.

Howling wisps of icy wind
And crunching sprigs of heather.
Soon to be knee-deep in snow,
Oh why can't it stay forever?

Jenny Parkin (13)
The Kingsway School

Runaway

Watching my whole life pass before my eyes while I was:
Running, running, running.
Not knowing where I was going.
Everything was blurry,
For my eyes were full of tears.
Pushing people out of my way,
I can hear the calling of my dear old mother,
She doesn't want me to go.
But I keep running,
I cannot stop.
What will come next?
Only time will tell.
I stop, tears streaming down my face,
Thinking of the life I once had.
Is it worth going back?

Abbie Gibson (11)
The Kingsway School

Winter

Long, cold, dark nights
Everywhere quiet.
A blanket of white lays on the ground
And snow falls on the hills.

Snow starts to fall
The birds fly away
Animals start collecting food
And then, they hibernate.

Frost on the grass,
Like a big spider's web.
Icy cold winds and
Frostbitten chins.

Benjamin Henderson (11)
The Kingsway School

Winter

As the cold dead night turns so much colder,
I shuffle and turn to pull my duvet to my shoulder.
Bang! the lights are out, I hold my teddy and give a little pout.

It's scary, it's frightening,
Oh no! here comes the lightning.
It's happening, I'm falling, falling asleep.

I look out the window and . . .
When the chilly skies turn into day
The winter snow is beginning to lay

Everything is as white as a whale's belly,
As sparkly as a rock,
It stings you with its bitterness,
And it can be as dangerous as a shark.

Nazanen Sadati (12)
The Kingsway School

My Autumn Wish

As I leave school the nights are dark,
Gone are the days I could play in the park.

The leaves are falling all around,
I kick as I walk through them on the ground.

The colours are bright, orange, yellow and brown,
They look crisp and beautiful all around.

The wind is blowing through the trees,
I pull my socks up over my knees.

I love to cuddle up in my duvet
And wish for the times I can go out to play.

Katie Collins (11)
The Kingsway School

Fallen Tree

Just lying there awaits a forest.
Full of sounds of its own residents,
Yet still we don't understand a thing they say.
Maybe not peaceful but not polluted by Man.

Not just this but some water speeds by.
Now just a stream but soon a mighty river.
The fish that struggle to dart through the gushes,
Have a glorious time to remember.

Scurrying away runs a small furry animal.
Holding its nut with so much precaution,
Because swooping near is a huge bald eagle.
Even though it's the least of their worries.

Walking nearby is a lumberjack.
Whispers of, 'It's him' take over the forest.
Emerges the dreaded axe ready to chop
Bang, it goes against the helpless tree.

Louder and louder, so unbearable,
He slices and cho-*bang* it falls
The birds fly away, the river stops,
For now the forest is finally silent.

Baber Uppal (11)
The Kingsway School

The Strong And The Weak

The grandmother sat down, tired,
Her aching bones creaking,
The children whispered,
Nervously at her feet,
As she started speaking.

'Now you lot settle down,
And hush as I speak,
I will tell you about the world,
About the strong and the weak.

The great Lord came upon us,
Showering us with life,
But we were too engrossed,
In our fears and our strife.'

The children were silent now,
Pondering if she knew,
Why water fell from the sky,
So the grass was wet with dew.

'We are very lucky here,
Because God has made us strong,
But there are many other people,
Who just want to belong . . .'

Charlotte Newton-Hale (11)
The Queen's School

The Cry Of The Icemark

A fierce battle,
Fatal surely!
No, we must have hope.
Be strong.
Be loyal.
Help save our country.
Blood! Blast and fire!
The cry of the icemark.
Alas the saviour's come:
The wolf-folk,
Vampires
And wood monarchs.
The leopards roar,
The wood monarchs charge,
The vampires screech,
The wolf-folk howl.
Rejoice? No
Regret.

Georgina Bolwell (11)
The Queen's School

Mountain

The mountain's summit looms high above the world
As it dominates the trees below and warns the clouds above
Of what is yet to come: a persistent battle against the frost.
It looks down at the frozen lake and wonders to what it plays witness,
For time is cruel yet cold is crueller as it removes the giver of life.
The trees reach out their arthritic fingers as they venerate their almighty mount,
Which has the power to stop the pain, the suffering,
Obliterate the torment. All fear the mountain, a few
Hundred feet up; raised high above the ground.
Did it take so long to grow if mountains could be sprung?
The snow, once so soft and gentle as it fell lightly to the ground,
Is now austere and bleak; there is no joy in it any more,
Where the children used to play in their bobble hats and coloured
Scarves, bringing the classic brown paper bag containing the
Traditional carrot's nose
And seed for the robin who is long since deceased.
However, the mountain that seems so scintillating and
Daunting at first, is but a mere grain of sand compared
To his elder brother, the volcano, yet as birds caw over
His purple caps, he speculates at his unimportance, at his
Insignificance to the world. And he looks below, upon
The frozen lake and he wonders to what the world is coming.
Yet, this scene a mere painting encased in a frame that holds, resilient,
In a cosy cottage in the middle of nowhere, where a crackling fire
Roars and spits, and where the mountain is but a few centimetres high.

Jill Evans-Higson (13)
The Queen's School

The Precious Pearl Is The Slave Of The Currents

A bleak sunset along the horizon, beckoning to me,
My boat wavering against the waves
Patterns twist and turn alongside of it.
Thinking always thinking . . .
What ages past, forgotten,
Time runs past like a wave of sins,
No beginning, no end as if elapsing into the past itself,
Foamy waves crash against the sandy dunes,
As earth, water and air interwine,
Where white horses leap and bound through the foamy waves,
The sunset is begging me now,
I'm picking up pace as I leap over the current,
I'm becoming one with the sea again as salty air glides past me now,
I feel my soul lift as I glide across the wonders of the misty blue,
I'm going . . . going. I'm . . . gone . . .

Elisabeth Welburn (11)
The Queen's School

Primrose

Primrose is a pussy cat
She lives inside my house
She likes to bring in rabbits,
And she also likes a mouse.

Voles, hedgehogs, rats and bluebirds,
She also likes to choose,
She brings them through the cat flap,
And hides them in Dad's shoes!

She likes to bring in bunnies,
To give to all my friends,
Her collection of little fluffy things
Never ever ends!

It's really quite surprising,
What Primrose likes to eat,
Last week she ate a *mammoth*
With great big hairy feet!

Katherine Lewis (11)
The Queen's School

The Fairies Gathering

They sing, they dance,
They spring, they prance,
It's the fairies out to play,
In their circle of mushrooms,
They dance around to the music while they sway.

With their long flowing hair,
And their delicate fluttering wings,
What beautiful dresses they wear,
Surrounded by wonderful things.

They spike their fingers,
They point their toes,
What wonderful singers,
As the song goes.

As night-time ends,
The fairies disappear,
And their song descends,
You would have no idea.

While the sun is up high,
You would not expect the fairies had been here,
This is the fairy gathering!

Helen Simmons (12)
Tytherington High School

The Last Time

Drifting up and up looking down on the daunting box
I was slumbering in.
Drifting up through clouds as soft as wool.
I see my life below me.

Being born and being cared for by my mother, but the clock ticks on,
No time to go back, I keep on going to see my first days at school,
All my friends, teachers, bullies.

Leaving them behind, blue skies above me, life below, I'm getting older
and bigger, faint but precious memories, meeting the love of my life
with a face like the sun and a spirit like the stars.

I see my wedding, my family and my friends and everyone smiling
And crying with joy,
My wife looking more beautiful than I'd ever seen her before,
But the pendulum swings on.

Travelling up to planets and stars, seeing my beautiful children growing
up and dark but happy funerals looking back at someone else's life not
thinking about mine.
But the bell chimes.

My face is withered and my hair is grey,
Playing with my grandchildren and watching like my grandparents
Watched me.
And the noises stop. Looking down on my funeral seems like a lifetime
ago, but just wanting to go back and tell everyone I'm OK
And I love them.
The clouds cover
I'm on my own.

Joseph Craig (12)
Upton High School

Time To Change . . .

I once knew a mermaid,
She had long red hair,
It was beautiful and gleaming.
Her sparkly tail shimmered in the sunlight.

I once knew a princess,
She had long blonde hair,
It was silky and shiny,
Her royal dress glistened in the moonlight.

I once knew a superwoman,
She had long black hair,
It was straight and smooth.
Her bold red cape blew in the wind.

I knew all these people,
Because they were me!
Who will I be next?
Let's wait and see . . .

Charlotte Parry (12)
Upton High School

I Cannot Be Heard

Roaring of fire,
Spreading like the hot butter on my toast.

A little boy walks past,
Crying for his parents,
And I run to my mother for comfort.

Buildings crashing to the ground,
As my baby brother knocks down his Lego tower,
And the pieces are scattered all over the floor.

The whining of sirens screams in my ear,
And I whisper, 'Ssshhhh'
But I cannot be heard.

Vanessa Ellis (12)
Upton High School

Seasons

Autumn leaves come falling down
Down down to the ground.
Some are red and some are green
Autumn makes a wonderful scene.

Winter nights long and cold
Fires burning bright and bold.
Pure white snow drifting down
Winter brings an eerie sound.

Spring blossoms blooming bright
Always make a wonderful sight.
Leaping lambs and newborn chicks
Mother Nature's worked her tricks.

Summer holidays, hip, hip, hooray
All the children out to play.
Summer sun burning bright.
A sunset glow brings on the night.

Lucinda Dodd (12)
Upton High School

Dark Waters

In a wash of gloom,
The darkness seems almost warm,
With small lights dotted over the midnight sea,
Feeling happiness glow inside me,
Just to know there was some life,
In the bright boats silhouetted,
Against the deep never-ending fog,
The moon reflecting over the softly lapping waves,
As ferries sail back and forth,
Holding tranquil passengers,
While other observers watch on,
As dark waters under me conceal beautiful creatures,
I gaze on in peace.

Katherine Burt (12)
Upton High School

Go-Karting

Sitting in the go-kart
Waiting for the instructor,
I listened to everyone's engine,
Revving and ready to go,
Finally the instructor shouted, 'Go!'
I pressed my foot down,
And off I went,
Whizzing past people,
Laughing and jerking round bends,
I heard the sound . . . zoom,
All my hair blowing in my face,
I was flying around the corners,
Lap after lap
'Stop!' shouted the instructor
We all slowed down
Screeched to the finish.

Chloe Seville (13)
Upton High School

Water Polo Spain Style

Blue and white splashes,
Of water flying around,
When I catch the ball,
I can only see a gang of heads swimming towards me
I throw the ball,
As far as I can,
People launching themselves
Around to catch the ball,
As I look at the water
I can see an orange reflection
Of the hot sun,
I hear the children shouting,
'Pass, pass, I'm free, I'm open,'
While their parents bathe their feet in the deep blue wavy water
While saying well done, keep on going.

Gareth Lilley (13)
Upton High School

Lanzarote

A bright summer's day
On the way to Lanzarote
Not a cloud in sight
The sun blazing down
The car sweltering
We get to the airport
We see a plane right over our heads
The noise of the plane deafening us
We approach the dropping off tunnel
All you see and hear are trolleys, suitcases and people shouting.
Now in the airport
Mum and Dad searching the boards for our check in desk
The check-in desks were hectic
We go through to the foyer, walk into a shop and tills making
                                                                their noise

Our flight is called, we walk through
I see an Aston Martin DB9
My brother stands there with his jaw dropped
My mum says, 'We're going to be late,'
So he runs to where Dad is
The flight is boarding
The pilot introduces himself over the intercom
The air hostess indicates left, right and centre
We're lining up to take off
Mum hates this bit
She closes her eyes
Frightened to death
I fall asleep on flight
I felt the seat shudder
It was scary
We arrived at the airport
All you see is welcome.
'We're here,' says my brother.

Alex Perratt (13)
Upton High School

Forest Adventure

Hiking up a mountain in Beddgelert.
I'm standing in front of a sea of green.
I look to the sky and see pine trees that seem to pierce the sky
Other trees sway like a flag in the wind.
Bushes rustle with life
The birds' song like background music.
The whole forest sounds like a full orchestra
Playing the peaceful melody
The path leads into the divine beyond
The trees lean over the path creaking an archway
I go deeper into the forest
Collapsed trees for me to venture over.
Deeper and deeper I go
The path starts to disappear before my eyes.
With no more path I must create my own.
I look up and the mountain face stares right back
I find what looks like an old house
Half of it has gone.
The ivy vines gripping to it like hands of green
I look up once again.
The light dapples through the trees
As if it's all trying to get through at once
I walk further and the forest seems to open into a pool of light.
I run forward.
It feels I have just walked through a portal of dark to light
I have reached the end of my journey
It feels like I have just walked into a painted canvas
I am standing on top of a rock face looking down over a lake
The lake reflects everything that surrounds it.
You can't see where the land ends and the sky begins.
I look back down into the forest
I say to myself, 'Another adventure awaits.'

Oliver Barnett (13)
Upton High School

I Had A Dream!

My bedroom was dark,
As the light went out.
I then fell asleep,
And awoke in a dream.
I was floating up and up in the dark sky,
Upon a white fluffy cloud.

I got up and there I was,
Looking through a tower window.
And there was a young girl,
With long blonde hair, with lovely blue eyes.
Sitting in her room,
Playing with her china dolls.

The room was pink and white,
With a cream four poster bed.
She was sitting on a furry lilac rug,
In the middle of the room.
She had a beautiful chandelier hanging from the ceiling.

She had four dolls all made out of china,
The young girl was redressing them.
They were all dressed in posh gowns,
Two pink, two blue, all ready for a ball.
I started to float back down,
And ended up back in bed fast asleep.

Leah Lipscombe (12)
Upton High School

A Light Of Colours

Everything went dark as I closed my eyes,
I fell deeply asleep.
I dreamt of floating up to a window,
Leaving my body in bed still asleep.

When I reached the window,
I saw myself walking to a lake.
Shivering as I walked,
I sat down in front of the waterfall.
I was fiddling with a pebble,
Suddenly a bright light shot over the waterfall.
I quickly jumped up,
Everything went so bright.
Even the sun came out,
I looked at the waterfall.
A band of colours was sparkling over it,
Dull colours I've seen for a long time.
Until today I know
I've seen the *light of colours!*

Hasna Ali (12)
Upton High School

Noises

The noises are getting louder,
As I get nearer to the door,
I can see shadows,
Moving in the room.

I hear voices,
Not a language I know,
Sounds strange,
Unearthly.

I hold my breath,
They don't know I'm there,
I take another step,
Another step towards the door.

Slowly I push it open,
The noises stop,
The only noise I can hear,
Is silence.

I put my head around the door
A bright light hits my eyes,
I look around,
The room is empty.

Rachael Brierley (13)
Upton High School

Ballet

I was lying in my bed,
Then I fell asleep,
I awoke into a long dream,
I dreamt I was at my window.

As I looked out I saw a beautiful room,
Painted pink and white,
With mirrors on the wall,
And inhabited by elegant dancers.

They were wearing pink leotards,
And big fluffy tutus,
With little satin shoes,
And a neat bun in their hair.

They were all in the middle,
Doing a pretty ballet dance,
Springing
And skipping around.

There was a girl I knew,
But I couldn't think who.

When I woke back up
I remembered she was me!

Natasha Hickson (12)
Upton High School

South African Arrival

Getting off the plane felt good to stretch your legs,
So many noises and colours as you walk in the airport,
People rushing to collect their bags and depart,
The noises of the rushing cases made nice rolling sounds,
All the speakers announcing the same thing.

Then you hear your name,
You look up and your family is there,
You haven't seen them in ages,
You take your first steps outside and you are blinded by the sun,
The noises of the cars and workers are so loud
You could be deafened.

You're in the car and leaving the airport,
You start seeing places that you can remember from years ago,
Somethings have and haven't changed.

The colours and noise make your stomach feel like butterflies
Are trying to escape,
As the night approaches you think that you are at home,
And you don't want to leave.

Byron Forster (14)
Upton High School

When I Was A Child

When I was a child lively and small,
I looked up to others and wished to be tall.
I played and I laughed all through the day,
But I screamed and shouted when I didn't get my way.
I completely ignored my chores and labours,
And climbed up a tree to spy on the neighbours.
Everything I owned just had to be pink,
And I'd wash my dolls' hair in the bathroom sink.
Dresses with bows was all I would wear,
And I wouldn't go anywhere without my fuzzy stuffed bear.
Dad would do magic and pull a coin out of my ear,
And we'd sit and watch football and drink blackcurrant juice and beer.
Mum would read me stories until she was blue in the face,
And dress me up for a ball in sequins and lace.
Bedtime would come, 'Upstairs,' Mum said,
So I'd say my goodnights and climb up to bed.
I'd drift into a dream feeling light as a feather,
And thinking, *I wish I could be a child forever.*

Mia Gatward (13)
Upton High School

Body Boarding

I was riding the waves!
I was actually doing it.
It felt great!
Then the nose of the board dipped.
I went with it.
I got salty water in my eyes.
In my mouth as well!
Then up my nose.
It was horrible.
I tried it again.
But this time I went under before the board.
It hit me in the back of the head.
I tried and tried and tried
But I couldn't do it!
I was getting fed up.
I thought of giving up.
But I tried it again
And I got it.
I felt amazing.
But it was getting dark.
Time to go
I was just enjoying it as well.

Ian Wilson (13)
Upton High School

Owl

I am a bird rushing through the cold night air
Waiting for prey
Turning my head this way and that.

Watching with my big blue eyes
Turning, waiting, watching,
I fly at speed up to a branch
On a tree in a wood.

Turning, waiting, watching
I hear a rustle down below
My eyes lock on
I swoop down like an aeroplane
Diving from the sky
Closing in on the target.

I make a strike with my razor-sharp talons
Digging into my prey
I am a hunter fast and strong
Turning, waiting, watching.

James White (12)
Upton High School

My Ghostly Visitor

I was asleep in bed
It was 2.35
When I felt a cold breeze
It was bitter on my face.

Then I could feel someone
At the head of my bed
Just playing with my hair
I was frozen to the bone.

It was a small girl ghost
With long, brown, plaited hair,
With big, sad, greyish eyes
Wearing a long white nightie.

'Hello?' I whispered, 'What's wrong?'
Then she suddenly screamed
'I couldn't save him Mum!
I've let you down . . . I did try . . .'

'What? What did you say?'
'The fire, I couldn't help . . .'
'Help what? What fire? Tell me . . .'
'The fire . . .! Timmy was trapped . . .
The year was 1806 . . .

I was in my bedroom
Mother told me not to . . .'
'Not to do what?'
'To never play with matches . . .'

She sniffed and then vanished
And a cold breeze blew past . . .

Lauren Riley (12)
Upton High School

Christmas

I turn the key
This time my hand is
The shield to the glorious sight,
This precious
Ark.

Like a child I cannot
Wait to see the
Swirling plumage
Of red and
Green.

And, like a child the
Curious innocence
Hastens me forward
Ever so silently
Creeping, creeping towards the
Scene.

A switch is flicked and
I look up;
All at once it is there
The beauty of it
Surprising me as much as the
Shimmering bauble that always manages to
Shatter.

But it is still on the tree
Anticipation growing,
Like the millions surrounding it
The red, gold and green
Blur holding such bright specks:
Christmas.

Alexandra Terry (17)
Upton High School

A Day As My Dog

I wake up at 9am
Come downstairs to my breakfast,
Butcher's lamb,
My favourite.

I walk out into the garden,
Scare away the pigeons,
And jump on the garden chair and wait for the postman.
Woof, woof,
The postman drops the letters and runs away,
I then fetch the letters in.

Then Lewis says one of my favourite words,
'Walkies,'
I jump onto the armchair,
Lewis puts on my lead,
We get into the car,
To Sandy Lane.

A place where lots of dogs go,
A vast field I run up and down,
With a river to drink and swim in.

We are getting close,
I can smell the water,
I put my head out of the car window.
I can't wait.

We finally get there,
My friends Millie and Duke are waiting for me,
We play all day long
Racing, catching and swimming,
We chase ducks until it is time to go.

Then it is back home,
For tea,
Beef and water,
Lovely.

Then it is into the front room,
I curl up to Lewis and watch television,
I slowly shut my eyes and go to sleep.

I wake up,
And play with Lewis,
Tug of war,
Fetch and races.

When it is finally time to go to bed,
Me and Lewis run upstairs,
Climb into bed,
I slowly close my eyes and dream of the past day,
Till morning I will sleep.

Lewis Whitehouse (12)
Upton High School

Panic

Slow, slow, slow.
The sloth moved through the trees,
Slow, slow, slow.
He clambered through the canopy,
Slow, slow, slow.
He hears the call of the white eagle,
Slow, slow, slow.
He musters all his speed.
Panic, panic, panic.
He hides in a hole in the tree trunk,
Panic, panic, panic.
The white eagle swoops like a bullet,
Panic, panic, panic.
All danger passes.
Slow, slow, slow.
The sloth carries on with his journey.

George Welsh (12)
Upton High School

Trapped

Floorboards screeching, doors squeaking
The drops of water pitter-pattering on the floor
You can see a shadow, 'Who is there?'
You say, no one answers.

The rats are rushing past you
Beside your feet,
A cat comes up to you and hisses
There it is, the shadow again, heading towards the kitchen.

You follow it, not knowing what you're doing
You hear the smashing of glass
Is that the whistling of a kettle?
Or your imagination?

You're scared, the drips
Of water are getting faster
You can hear footsteps heading towards you
Someone screams,
'Who's there?' you say again.

The shadow is there, moving towards you now
You start to run down the stairs and out of this nightmare!
The footsteps are getting louder and faster but there
You are at the front door, you turn around there's the
Shadow but not a shadow a real man! He's carrying a knife
And staring at you right in the eye!

Daniel Preston (12)
Upton High School

Crying People

Tears, tears of love, tears of fear,
People crying and I never knew why.
I just stood there looking at them
Tears running down their faces.

If I thought about it, I was alone,
A room of crying people and I didn't know any of them.

Why were they crying?
What were those tears for?

These people crying everywhere
The devastation on their faces,
Looking up from the floor for only a second.

People lonely and filled with anger,
People celebrating
Their faces lit up with joy.

A wedding, such a happy time!

Where was I?

A church.

Imogen Rhodes (12)
Upton High School

The Plague!

Misty streets dripping with fear
Children grieving for family and friends.
As their close companions disappear
They don't know when their time will end.

Day by day the illness grows
Hits each town with a bloodthirsty bite.
While many people's hearts froze
The streets were always a horrible sight.

The days were as dark as night.
Red crosses spread on every door.
The plague was like a battle to fight
But most of us lost, and fell to the floor.

Later when all were tucked away
A low sounding bell hit the air
'Bring out your dead,' a voice would say,
So all we could do was get up and stare.

Francesca Walton (12)
Upton High School

Destination Solar System

Go past the fiery sun,
Turn left at small Mercury,
Sharp right at cloudy Venus.

Avoid the meteorites!

Zoom over the Earth,
Speed past red Mars,
Go round big Jupiter.

Dodge the black hole!

Go under ringed Saturn,
Bend round rocky Uranus,
Swerve past icy Neptune.

Now you have toured the Solar
System return to your
Departure
Point.

Ellie Liddell-Crewe (12)
Upton High School

Blade

B ullets are firing, Blade's arriving
L ights flicker and vampires bicker
A utomatics loaded, all doors coded
D oomsday's arriving, death or demise
E nemies surround him, everyone's around him.

Martin Clarke (11)
Verdin High School

The Stage

I've always wanted to be on the stage
It has always been my dream
But when I actually got a part
It wasn't what it seemed!

I wanted to sing and strut my stuff
Be the prima donna
But I had to be the elephant's bum,
I knew I was a goner!

The great day came, the curtain went up
My parents thought I was the lead
If they ever found out the real truth
They would be ever so peeved.

It was great I came on
All was going well
Until I fell apart and was revealed!
Then the curtain fell!

Emily Pointon (12)
Verdin High School

Trick Or Treat

Scary faces
Dark fright
Full moon drifting above the Devil's night.
Creepy noises
Decorated houses
With a shiver of fear
Better get running, midnight is here
He's coming
He's coming.

Trick or treat?

Mark Robson (11)
Verdin High School

In The Dark

In the dark
You don't know where you are
In the dark
There are monsters and aliens in a racing car.

In the dark
There are ghouls
In the dark
There are mindless zombie fools.

In the dark
Where you can't see
In the dark
Your imagination runs free
In the dark
Just maybe.

Adam Smith (12)
Verdin High School

My Mum

To you her name is Di
She went to meet the Queen
To me her name is Mam, the best
You have ever seen.

She works very hard
She stays over time
We are very, very proud
How she finds the time
Mum you are so brilliant
You're kind and loving too
We don't know what we'll do without you
Because that's my mum for you.

Yasmin Woodward (11)
Verdin High School

Friends Until The End!

This poem is for my special friends,
I hope they're my friends until the end!

I will tell you about each of them,
Yet there is only three,
If you are lucky I might even tell you some,
Secrets that they've shared with me.

The oldest out of the lot is my friend Shannon G,
She really is a great friend as kind as can be!
But a few times she has done something that really hurt me,
It hurts inside though, not the outside, as it's something you
                                             can't see!

But other than that she truly is a great friend to me!
I hope we are always friends, friends until the end!

The second oldest of them is a friend I have had,
For longer than all the rest, knowing she's there really makes
                                             me glad,
Her name is Jade Dickinson and when she sees I am sad,
She is always there to cheer me up and calm me down when I
                                             am mad.
I hope we are always friends, friends until the end!

The third oldest is another Shannon, and indeed another girl,
She is pretty, kind and funny and she will gladly give you an
                                             elegant twirl,
She is really funny and pretty with her lovely little curls,
I really think she is a very, very friendly girl,
And indeed I hope we will always be friends, friends until the end!

So they all are my three friends,
Very special friends,
I truly hope they all are,
My friends until the end!

Danielle Harris (11)
Verdin High School

Serious Sam

Serious Sam from Scun
Who decided to pull out his gun
He blew off the head
And the monster was as good as dead.

He went to the planet of Zarr
And got in his space car
He was told to blow up the monster base
But failed and got chased by the whole monster race.

They chased him so fast
Surely this fast pace couldn't last
He hoped they would get tired
Or into the air he would be fired.

He jumped and he ran then climbed the highest tree
He prayed from up high that the monsters would not see
The monsters all went rumbling fast
He hoped he would be free of them at last.

This was a bad idea, the monsters should be left as they are
He wished he was back at home which at this moment seemed oh

so far.

He came down from the tree and in the ground was a dip
Which hopefully was the one where he left his spaceship.

He turned the key and the engines did roar
Just as the monsters came banging at the door
He was glad to be on his way home
And thankfully on his ship he was alone.

Ben Littlemore (11)
Verdin High School

The Feelings Of Heaven

Where my heart lies,
When the happiness dies,
Through the fun and the joy,
I hear the cries,
Of sadness.

Feelings of sorrow,
It'll be there tomorrow,
Nobody's there,
My heart is hollow,
Because of loneliness.

Shiver and gaze,
Where are all the days,
I'm frightened to death,
In so many ways,
It's scary.

The pathway is clear,
Follow my dear,
It's shining and golden,
I've lost all my fears,
My head is empty.

I hear a bell,
But not in Hell
Not family or friends
It's I who fell
Into Heaven.

I look down
I see my old town,
My family and friends,
Cry and frown,
Over me.

Samantha Lyon (11)
Verdin High School

Stuck!

Stuck in my room
Trying to break free,
Want to see the world,
To become what I dream.

Reach for the stars,
Believe in yourself,
You have the strength
No need for help.

Your dreams are real
Live them out,
So shout to the world
'Let me out!'

To speak to people,
I want to meet
And inspire people
To let their possibilities break free.

Just to look up and see the stars
Realise they're not that far.

I want to be a drifting star,
Looking down to the Earth below
So I'm telling you please
Let me go!

Molly Grogan (11)
Verdin High School

Love

Love is a thing that can't go away
It stays with you every day.

It makes you happy
When things seem down
And it *never* makes you frown.

Kayleigh Daniels (12)
Verdin High School

Dragons

Dragons, dragon, in the air,
Shooting fire everywhere,
Red-hot fire from the tum
Sometimes coming out the bum.

Red hot gases in the air
Dragon flying pair by pair
Dragon wings gold and red
See how fast the fire spreads.

Their eyes are like rubies covered in flame,
They look like they're encrusted
Sometimes they're sapphires, sometimes they're black
They look so fierce, they're as tall as a skyscraper
They are as dark as a grave, black as their shadow
But that doesn't matter because they're back in town.

Jade Vernon & Warrick George (11)
Verdin High School

Stripy

Stripy was our beloved cat,
With the most gorgeous stripes you will ever see
The vet said his teeth were perfect and he was so beloved.

I came home on Sunday evening,
He was gone, not there, disappeared,
He'd had blood clots and was put down
I never got to say goodbye
He was gone, not ever coming back.

So as the famous saying goes: you never realise
How much you love something till it's gone.

Emily Baddeley (11)
Verdin High School

My Liverpool FC

My Liverpool FC,
the best team as can be.
Who could argue when we've had Kenny D?
We don't just cheer when we're at the top,
we are always singing from the Kop.
With five European Cups
and eighteen leagues,
we're better than United, Pompey and Leeds.
At Istanbul 2005 we beat Milan when we were 3-0 behind.
So you can see,
Liverpool FC will always be the best team for me.

Jacques Vincent (11)
Verdin High School

Liverpool

L iverpool are the one to love
I ncredible they are
V ery clean they are
E very match they try to beat the best
R ampaging through the rest and the best
P eople in the crowd cheering loud
O i Liver, do us proud
O ver their heads the ball goes in
L ucky for us we're going to win.

Kavan Farrell (11)
Verdin High School

Sadness

Sadness is a dull time
Sadness is when you don't want to be alone
All you need is family and friends around
To try and make you happy again.

Kelly Davenport (13)
Verdin High School

My Dog

My dog is number one
She is pretty and pleasant
'Cause she is my dog
Soft, gentle, kind and loving.

She may be old
But age doesn't matter
She will always be my puppy dog.

Coming home to a warm welcome
Licking my face and giving me a kiss
She is always there for me
She will always be my number one dog.

Maybe some day she will have gone for others
However, she will always be there for me.

Chloe Sharrock (11)
Verdin High School

Cabin Boy

'Up with the anchor,' the Captain says,
Out of the port we go.
Off to sail the seven seas
Off to explore the world
From Europe to Asia
From Africa to Australasia.
I'm going to travel the Earth
Beep, beep, beep.
I wake with a start, a shock, a jolt,
In the ship's cabin quarters,
For I am the cabin boy.

Molly Carroll (11)
Verdin High School

My Emerald Dragon

In the cave in my house
A dragon lives.
At night is the time he shifts.

His eyes are huge light orbs,
His scales huge emerald sheets,
His wings are flaming sunshine beams,
His teeth are daggers of steel.
My emerald dragon.

At night he eats,
Fire burning from his tummy,
He eats lamb every night,
From a farmer called Llewelyn.

That is my emerald dragon,
The best friend in the world!

Elliot Orme (11)
Verdin High School

It!

It lay there under my bed,
I didn't dare look but I knew it was there.
It was an awful silence,
Its heartbeat was like thunder *boom, boom.*
It started to scramble to its feet,
A shiver ran down my spine.
A drip of sweat ran down my red face,
Then my dad came to me,
He sat with me.
The next night I listened for it nervously,
It wasn't there,
I thought,
Would I ever see it again?

Chloe Bell (11)
Verdin High School

Monsters Under The Bed

I'm lying there in my bed
Thinking of the rising dead
What about the zombie man
Come and catch me if you can.

I hear a shriek,
Do I dare to peek?
What can it be?
Is it coming after me?

I had a dream
What can it mean?
I saw a ghost
At a gate post.

I can't wait for the morning
When the sun is dawning
When I go to school
Away from the ghouls.

Daniel Munro (11)
Verdin High School

The Haunted House

I hear the floorboards click and squeak
I can smell the rustiness on the rusty door
I can see the cracked windows about to fall
I am touching the bashed and broken gate
I can taste the thick dust and the taste of fear
Beware, beware of the house right here
There are *spooky* things that gives you *fear!*

Jessica Hughes (12)
Verdin High School

Anger

Anger is mad
But inside you are sad
It turns you bad
Get help from Dad!

Anger from lads
Is especially bad
They wind you up
And make you mad!

Charlotte Ellis (11)
Verdin High School

The World

I love to sing and play guitar
M iniature people from so far
A nd all things beautiful
G reen, yellow, purple and brown flying all around
I n and out that gorgeous sound
N othing better to do
E njoying the sound and colours bright.

Jack Oakes (11)
Verdin High School

Forever Sparkling Bright

The sun is gleaming in the soft blue sky,
The moon is shining in the thick black night,
The two together are as bright as diamond earrings,
How wonderful they are jointly gleaming.

Emily Williams (11)
Verdin High School

My Mum

My mum is so the best,
She's prettier than all the rest,
When she goes out she looks so fine,
When she comes in she's out of her mind
There's something about my mum (I know what)
She properly lost the plot,
When she smiles her teeth are so bright,
They even dim down to the light.
When I kiss her smooth lips
And she gives me all her tips
I love her so much.
I love her so much
And I know that
That's why I love her.

Leann Brown (12)
Verdin High School

Trick Or Treat?

It's Hallowe'en night
Am I in for a fright?
A knock at the door,
A creak on the floor.
Outside is a sound,
I look all around
Just then a crunch of stones
It chills me to the bones
What can it be
Should I go and see?
As I open the door
And I explore
Who do I meet?
Some kids, 'Trick or treat?'

Jarrod Pickering (11)
Weaverham High School

Mountain Biking

Hill approaching
Muscles tiring
Gears grinding
Cogs rotating
Frame creaking
Energy dwindling
Summit reached
Downhill beginning
Wheels spinning
Forks suspending
Eyes straining
Adrenaline pumping
Wind howling
Brakes boiling
Tyres screeching
Mud splattering
Hands tensed
Puncture hissing.

That's what mountain biking is for me.

Chris Dilnot (11)
Weaverham High School

Hallowe'en

H allowe'en trick and treat
A ll the sprites come to live
L ots of fun
L ots of sweets
O pen your imagination
W ild as wild can be
E at lots of sweets
E njoy the fun
N ever forget Hallowe'en.

Will & Sam Monson (12)
Weaverham High School

The Cave

Darkness caves in all around,
He is under the ground,
Already imagining his grave,
The deadly silence is setting in,
The hope of life is thin.

Chills run down his spine
Whilst he climbs mountainous stone hills,
Ice-cold water drops
Whilst in his mind rolls a dice, choosing his fate
Unfortunately, his time alive dims.

Fear steps up a gear, teasing his mind,
He starts to cry as he knows time is passing by.

Just before hope was broke, he could see darknesses end,
Dread was no longer ahead for now he was safe.

Luke Basnett (11)
Weaverham High School

A Poem About Light

It's warm glow spreads around the room,
The candle's flame spreading calm,
Moving side to side creating warm.
In the dark the candle's glowing,
In the breeze the candle's blowing,
Around the room reflecting light,
Transforming dull into bright.
Twinkling and sprinkling away.

Gemma Craven (11)
Weaverham High School

From Hallowe'en To Christmas

There was once a ghost from Hallowe'en
Who had accidentally been
To Christmas!
And this is what he said,
Once out of his bed!

I had a dream,
That I was sucked up a beam,
To a land they called Christmas.

There were children throwing snowballs,
Instead of throwing heads
People decorating their walls
And of course their beds!

The ghost's name was Jack
No one in Hallowe'en believed him
So he decided to go back.
Crash!
He landed back
And hurt his back

No one in Hallowe'en ever saw him again!

Carys Tavener (11)
Weaverham High School

A Hallowe'en Night

H allowe'en, Hallowe'en
A scary night.
L ots of children trick or treating,
L aughing all through the night,
O therwise known as All Hallows Eve.
W hat scary costumes,
E ven vampires!
E verybody dressing up,
N obody ever hates it!

Olivia Done (12)
Weaverham High School

The Forest

Giant men of pine, oak or elm,
Reaching for the new day's sun,
Dewdrops shine like silver glass,
Leaves from trees bow down like slaves,
Pressed against the cold soft mud.

Streams dance and twirl,
Along the winding path,
Small curled hedgehogs like round pin cushions,
Hiding in the crisp, fragile leaves,
Owls search for their prey,
Listening for the slightest rustle,
Talons like a gripping hand.

Small brown mice,
Living in the rich foliage,
Scurrying, scattering,
Fleeing from the might of the snakes,
Silent predators,
Of venom and speed,
Like a shadow they hide away,
Waiting to attack.

But when the ice, snow and frost,
Comes to the forest,
Giants of pine stand bare and cold,
New day sun is dull and shadowed,
Crystallised dew shines like a diamond,
All leaves are frozen to the ground,
Cold and crisp as ever.

Streams no longer frolic and dance,
But are solemn and frozen,
Hedgehogs and owls hide from the frosty wrath of winter.
All the mice and snakes burrow,
Deep in safe havens of warmth and protection,
The frost consumes all in its icy path.

Melissa Brown (11)
Weaverham High School

Hallowe'en Night

The ghosts come out to play
But not during the day
The ghosts come out to play
Waiting all day.
The witch brews her cauldron
Waiting for the children
The witch brews her cauldron
Making her tea.
The zombies need to feed
Eating what they need
The zombies need to feed
Always eating weeds.

Liam Hampson (11)
Weaverham High School

Christmas Day

C hristmas is near
H ip hip hooray!
R udolph Red Nose pulls Santa's sleigh
I t's Christmas Day!
S now is like a woolly blanket
T rickling from the sky
M ums and dads get tipsy
A s the day goes by
S o much fun and happiness.

D oes everyone deserve
A nd now the day is nearly gone
Y uletide greetings to everyone.

Laura Foy (11)
Weaverham High School

The Darkness Of Hallowe'en

The light shone bright for the whole of the day,
But when darkness came it wasn't here to stay.
I feel safe when light is around,
I feel scared when the Devil comes out of the ground.
Time for bed and also time to be dead.
My hands shook with fright,
But I knew the Devil would stay for the night!
The dark shadow came out
While I was still up and about.
I did not know that I would be next,
It was written down in the Devil's text.

Mark Marafko (11)
Weaverham High School

The Sea

The sea is a graceful woman dancing in the waves
The sea is a roaring giant, crashing towards the shore.

The sea is a blue mass rolling to shining froth.
The sea is a merciless beast, drowning the bodies and
Souls of innocent people in her killing storms.

The sea is a caring nanny, giving homes to thousands of
Wonderful animals, taking all that need her into her care.
The sea is a whisper, gliding along the sand.
The sea is . . .

Rachel Trafford (12)
Weaverham High School

Trick Or Treat?

T rick or treat is fun,
R un around all night,
I t's fun to get treats and sweets,
C ould even sit by the fire eating chocolate
K ids love Hallowe'en dressing up
O r (if you're old) stay tight up in bed
R ing the doorbells, get sweets.

T rick or treating, great, but very scary,
R oads and streets full of monsters
E ating sweets as if it beats
A t parties people play games
T rick or treat, get out there, have some fun.

Sarah Gerrard (11)
Weaverham High School

Hallowe'en Time

H allowe'en is spooky
A pple bobbing for apples
L ots of sweets
L ots of laughter
O ld crooked witches
W icked wizards
E vil devils
E nd of Hallowe'en
N ightmare time.

Joe Dalton (12)
Weaverham High School

The Girl

On a stormy night there lay a girl
Whom no one had seen before.
She slept on the floor as if in a bed
Though her bed was mossy wood instead.

Out of the dark there came a wolf,
Growled, barked and licked his lips.
The young girl was startled,
She began to run but there was no way out!

The sun came out, the wolf disappeared,
The girl was saved again.
Skipped and danced her way home,
Thanks to light happiness came.

Jessica Dean (11)
Weaverham High School

Hallowe'en

H allowe'en makes me think of
A pple bobbing
L oads of children trick or treating
L ollipops in my bag
O ut at night on Hallowe'en
W itches cackling, bats flying
E vil witches out at night
E ating sweets and counting money
N ightmares are coming our way.

Natasha Jackson (12) & Amanda Harris
Weaverham High School

The Sea

The sea is like horses galloping,
Demolishing anything in their path.
As the waves crash, a burst of creamy white foam
Spreads the ocean like a chocolate fountain.
When the sea is rough the current drags boats into a deathtrap
Swallowing them up like a monster.
Sailors fall to their death petrified and go down,
Down to the belly of the beast where they decide your fate,
Whether you should lie or die.
If you go down to the bottom of the sea
You should never close your eyes
Because if you do,
You will fall into your dreams
And you won't be able to escape them.

Oliver Timmins (11)
Weaverham High School

Black Cats

Black cats, with silky black fur,
Black cats, that sleep and purr.
Black cats, that hunt deep into the night.
Black cats that give you a fright!

Black cats that have amber eyes,
Black cats that sneak and hide,
Black cats that prowl the house,
Black cats that wait for a mouse.

It's now the end of black cat's day,
Now he will wait for another time to play.

Lucy Moulton (11)
Weaverham High School

Night And The Wolf

At night the wind howls,
It bites you and is extremely bitter.

Night is dangerously dark
The most danger happens.

The wolf howls at the shiny moon,
And the sea is as shimmery as a bed of diamonds.

The people are hid away in their houses,
They are tucked up in a blanket
By the warm fire,
Whilst the wolf is sleeping in the bitter coldness.

The wolf howls
Howls
Howls
Until it's morning.

Sarah Koch (11)
Weaverham High School

Christmas Eve

C hristmas presents under the tree
H appy faces on you and me
R unning around on the last day
I ce drops dancing at the end of your noses
S now making the rooftops white
T onight is the night of all nights
M erry faces as friends and family reunite
A cold winter's day
S now getting trod into our warm, cosy houses

E veryone excited
V ery excited faces
E veryone determined not to go to bed.

Farrah Hallworth (12)
Weaverham High School

Hallowe'en Frights

H ats and masks
A ll very scary, pumpkins are alight
L ooking for sweets and chocolate
L ooking for sweets and chocolate to eat in the dark night
O pen the door and you see the sweets
W hen you take them you want some more
E ven more than anyone else
E ven more than everyone else!
N o one shall get the sweets now I've got them.

F rightening costumes lurking in the night
R ound the corner, left and right
I n front of you and behind you
G etting closer and closer
H ere they are
T hey're only little children dressed up
S o many of them but they're only children.

Will Jordan (11)
Weaverham High School

Hallowe'en Night

H allowe'en is coming
A ll the scary costumes
L ittle children dressing up
L ike ghosts, ghouls, witches and skeletons
O h they're so scary
W e all get sweets together
E verywhere's dark
E vening has come
N ight-time's upon us, everyone run.

N o, I'm not scared
I really am not
G o away ghosts
H urry up go
T oni has now finished the show.

Toni Woodward (11)
Weaverham High School

The Shadow

It was a dark, stormy night.
The boy was scared of thunder outside.
He closed his eyes hoping he would fall asleep.
And he fell asleep.
A shadow put his creepy hand round the door.
The boy was still asleep.
The shadow crept in.
His fangs were dripping.
Drip, drip, drip.
The shadow came in closer, closer, closer.
The shadow was unaware of dawn appearing.
The shadow decided to launch his fangs into the boy.
A gust of wind blew the curtains.
The sun burst into the room.
The shadow scurried away.
The boy was saved by the sunlight.

William Corradine (11)
Weaverham High School

The Creeps

In a house far away
Lives a zombie wrapped away
In a coffin near the stairs
Stand on air all his hair.

Slamming open the coffin door
Coming out to scar some more
Chasing down the hall I ran
Being followed by a crazy man.

Running down the alleyway
To the graveyard far away
Coming up close I let out a scream
I sat up in bed, it was only a dream.

Shaun Scott (13)
Werneth School

My Space Trip

I'm sat there, at NASA,
Cup of coffee in hand,
Rather nervous about my trip,
Getting into Alien Land!

I'm sat there in my seat,
Wearing my spacesuit,
The rocket starts to sway,
5, 4, 3, 2, 1, we're awaaay!

So, I'm floating through space,
Enjoying the starry view
When *swoosh!* An alien flies up to me
-      actually quite a few.

They ask me where I am from
And what I'm up to
Only to find out later
They catch me and make me
Into stew!

Jessica Porter (12)
Werneth School

Ted The Alien!

As I was watching TV
My mum came and said
'Outside there is an alien called Ted
He has a blue face with spots
And a body that's stuck with knots.'

I went outside to check it out
And found him stuck in the spout
I yanked him out with a hud and a thud
And then fell in a pile of mud
I have got to know him really well
But *shh* please don't tell.

Alex Moore (12)
Werneth School

The Lonely House

Years and years go by,
But there is no one around.
And no one by.
The wind blows an eerie sound.
The tree branches creak really loud.
The sky grows darker and darker.
This is a night like all nights.
Sometimes it rains, sometimes it doesn't
Who gives a care, I'm only a house!

Sometimes I pray there is someone around.
But all there is, is a little black cloud.
I saw a bird the other day.
But I scared it away.
Am I really that ugly?
Is that why no one likes me?
I will never know why.
Because I am lonely
But I realised that I am not.
I have a friend in the house . . .

A ghost.

Lauren Baguley (12)
Werneth School

Creepy Zombies

In a house so tall and thin
There was a zombie in a bin
I saw it sleeping I saw it then
I thought I'd scare it once again.

Then it jumped on top of me
I whizzed off quick like a bee
Behind a wall I had to dive
There I decided I would hide.

Rio Trowsdale (12)
Werneth School

The Evil Clown

The evil clown, oh that horrid giggle
Waiting at the carnival for its next victim
Holding that huge bloodstained knife
And then it strikes thud! the victim hits the floor.

The evil clown, the evil clown
Oh what a horrid sight
Its face of creepy paint and things
Then waiting for its next victim . . .

The evil clown, the evil clown
Its cherry-red nose shining like a siren
And its vest covered in thick bloodstains
Then it walks through its victims guts and mangled body.

The evil clown, the evil clown
Murders people for a laugh
But gets away every time
The evil clown, oh what a horrid sight.

Thomas Welton (13)
Werneth School

Space

I am on-board my ship,
With a cuppa on side,
I am rather excited for my trip to Earth Land!

Off we go I am jumping for joy,
I heard a bang, what could it be?
Maybe a rat, mouse or a bee,
We have finally landed with a bump and a bang,
Come tumbling off with a roll and a prang.

I loved the journey except for the bang
I have come to investigate and see what I can find.
I have found a house, what's inside?
I will go and have a look and keep what I find.

Alexandra Wilson (12)
Werneth School

The Chosen One

I was walking down the creepy street
And then I heard the nightmare beat
I really wanted to look around
But then I heard a chilling sound
I started to run down the street
With the moon glistened light by my feet
I kept on running for my life
And then I saw the blood dripped knife
I stared at the thing for quite some time
And then I heard a silver chime
I turned around and saw a ghost
I ran and I screamed at the top of my voice
I run and I fall flat on my face
And I can only walk at snail's pace.
I feel the floor through my shoes
This annoying ghost is hard to lose
I stop at the side to have a breath
And then I feel the touch of death
I jump around to turn and face
And then I see the gruesome disgrace
Me and the ghost were one to one
And then he held up the chosen one
As I look I see my face
And figure out I am the disgrace.

Bradley Walker (12)
Werneth School

At The Mansion

I could see a shadow at the bottom of the corridor,
I could hear big footsteps coming towards me,
I felt a really cold breeze, as the footsteps were getting faster,
I could smell a really bad stench from the end of the corridor,
I could taste my dinner coming back up my throat.

Sean Bowen (12)
Werneth School

Bestest Buddies

Sat in my ship
My spacesuit on
Going to Mars
To visit John.

He's red and blue
With three huge eyes
Hands like claws,
They're great in size.

He sounds pretty creepy
But he's not at all
As soft as a pillow
And he's really small.

He's my bestest friend
As good as gold
We'll be friends forever
Till we're grey and old.

Megan Burns (12)
Werneth School

Scary Fairy Cakes!

First add a cup of flour to make the mixture rise
Add a dash of brains to add some spice
And a sprinkle of gut to add some flavour.

Chop some eyes and add later
Add some grated dandruff to make it thick
Fold in some minging snot to add some colour

Take out the hearts and swirls, they'll make it girly
Replace it with blended fingers
Leave to settle for 15 mins
When done bake at 300°

Once done decorate with black icing
Your cake should look like this.

Toni Crosby (12)
Werneth School

The Vanishing At the Fair

I was at a fair in the middle of the night,
I went into the haunted house,
I was really scared because I heard the floorboards creak,
I looked behind me and the door locked,
Then I panicked,
I rushed to the window to try to get out,
But they all shut too,
So I kicked and kicked at the door,
I eventually got out then when I did . . .
Everyone had vanished.
'They could not have gone home,' I said,
'Cause I was only in there for a minute,
Then I thought,
It must be that spooky house,
So I went back out and everyone was there,
Flippin' eck I thought to myself.

Jake White (12)
Werneth School

My Spaceship

My spaceship has heaps of beeps,
It can move very smooth,
It can fly very high,
It does a weird hover but I don't really bother,
When the engine gets hot we need to stop,
My spaceship is coloured green but everyone thinks it looks unclean,
I am very unkeen because it puffs out a lot of steam,
When it's time for tea there will be someone
Calling a million miles away for me.

Bradley Fuller (12)
Werneth School

Toby The Ghost

My brother came and told me,
There is a ghost called Toby.
He transforms into a mouse,
And he lives in the haunted house.
I thought I should go and see it,
To the house where the candles lit.
As I turned the corner my face went very pale,
I looked at the house and saw a ghostly male.
I followed my brother up the hill,
Past the old dusty mill.
As we approached the freaky ghost,
He looked like a TV host.
I heard the ghost scream,
He loves custard creams.
I gave him none but,
He wanted one.
Toby's my best friend,
Friends forever till the end.

Katie Spencer (12)
Werneth School

Blue Bananza

On the spaceship I could see
My planet from far off.
I could smell the engine burning
I could feel my hands getting hot.
I could taste the warm tension
I could hear the sweat running down my face.

As I get out of my spaceship
I can see the aliens welcoming me
I can smell the relief of being at home again.
I can feel their excitement
Running through me.
I can taste the blue bananza air once again.
I can hear my heart beating with relief.

Coral Heavyside (13)
Werneth School

Alien

Its ears point
Its eyes scare
It has scraggly hair
There's an alien in England, beware!

Its jowels
Its spots popped
Its feet webbed
Slime slivering down its head.

Saliva dribbling off its tongue
Its antennae long
Its nails pointed
And its hands double jointed.

Its belly pot
Human it is not
Hobbled is how it walked
English is what it talked.

Amber Marsland (12)
Werneth School

We Are Not Alone

I was sat in the rocket
Waiting for the countdown
My captain said buckle up
5, 4, 3, 2, 1 now we were up.

We were shooting through the atmosphere
At 1000 miles per hour
I looked out of my window
There stood an alien.

I screamed, I shouted,
'There's an alien, there's an alien'
But everyone doubted me
I wished they would see.

The alien had four green toes
But a really big bogey nose
Suddenly all the buttons started flashing
Something must be going wrong.

Jake Francis (12)
Werneth School

Young Writers Information

We hope you have enjoyed reading this book - and that you will continue to enjoy it in the coming years.

If you like reading and writing poetry drop us a line, or give us a call, and we'll send you a free information pack.

Alternatively if you would like to order further copies of this book or any of our other titles, then please give us a call or log onto our website at www.youngwriters.co.uk

**Young Writers Information
Remus House
Coltsfoot Drive
Peterborough
PE2 9JX**

(01733) 890066